Diagonal Ties:

A family history in Wales and the North East of England

About the Author

 Susan Lewis CBE was born in County Durham and went to school in Billingham, Llanelli (briefly), and Hartlepool. She graduated from the University of Newcastle in the late 1960s. From there she went on to study education at the University of Sheffield.

Susan stayed in Yorkshire for the next 16 years, starting out as a science teacher and ending up in charge of a secondary school. In the mid-1980s, she turned gamekeeper by becoming a school inspector in Wales. Susan later became the first woman to be appointed as Her Majesty's Chief Inspector of Education and Training in Wales. She was awarded the CBE for services to education in 2008.

Susan currently lives in Cardiff. Since retiring, she has pursued her passion for growing plants to eat and look at. She enjoys cooking, sewing, painting and drawing. She has also worked out family trees for herself and friends and written a couple of books which reveal her roots in the North East and Wales.

Her first book, Home on the range: growing up on Teesside in the 50s and 60s, was published in 2011. Diagonal Ties: a family history in Wales and the North East of England is her second book.

Diagonal Ties:

A family history in Wales and the North East of England

by Susan Lewis

www.6epublishing.net

First published in paperback in 2013
by Sixth Element Publishing
Arthur Robinson House
13-14 The Green
Billingham TS23 1EU
Tel: 01642 360253

ISBN 978-1-908299-46-8

British Library Cataloguing in Publication Data. A catalogue record for this book is available from the British Library.

Printed in Great Britain.

www.6epublishing.net

For Tony

Contents

Introduction

Diagonal Ties is about family ties.

You will probably be attracted to this book if you are interested in family history, especially in the period 1740 to 1960. It could prove even more appealing if your roots are in Wales or the North East of England. If you have ancestors in both of these places then you have double the reason to carry on reading. If you or your ancestors are named Lewis, Thomas, Bird, Dixon, Francis or Newall then we might even be related, so do continue. If your family name is Foster, Benson, Sengelow or Turner then we too could be related via the wider Lewis line.

This book is the story of some of my ancestors set against the times in which they lived. The tale starts with rural Welsh life in the 1700s. It moves on into the heart of the industrial revolution in Wales and England. It shows how events, world, national, local and personal, affected the lives and fortunes of those concerned. You will travel with my family from land and money in Wales to a lonely death in the workhouse in the North East of England. You will trek with another family member to war in South Africa and live through the time of a riot in Wales, a general strike, and two world wars. The story ranges through the reigns of nine kings and queens as one person from each generation makes that diagonal journey that will determine whether he or she will live as a Welsh person or a North Easterner.

I grew up in the North East of England in the 1950s and 60s. In the way you do when you are young, I simply accepted what my life was like. But as I began to learn about my friends' families, I realised that my circumstances were a bit different from theirs. Different in that my mother had died when I was young and all of my grandparents had died long before I was born. My immediate family therefore only comprised my older brother and my father.

I knew my father was Welsh. He didn't speak like people around us, more especially when his sister and her husband came to stay with us. I knew my mother wasn't Welsh. I began to wonder why my parents had moved from their places of birth and how they had come to be together where we lived in the North East.

In common with most people who start tracing their family tree, I began my research with my own surname. Even though it is genetically absurd, I have always felt more connected with those who had the same surname as me. Perhaps this connection to the Lewises was exacerbated by the fact that my mother was not around long enough for her family to have had a direct influence on me.

Lewis: acknowledged in the UK as a Welsh surname. I read thirty years ago that it was the 11th most common name in the UK. When I last looked, it was 23rd and falling, so we have dropped back in the race to pass on our family name to future generations. As my brother only had daughters and I had no children, I suppose we must take our share of collective responsibility for this slipping in the Lewis genetic and ancestral leagues.

I began my research by asking my father and his two remaining sisters what they recalled of their parents and grandparents. Dad and his sisters told me differing tales of their mother and father. My father casually told me that his mother was an alcoholic. The eldest of his sisters would not hear of such a thing. My father thought his father was rather strict. His sisters said he was the kindest person they knew. They also recounted stories of their maternal grandmother who had lived with the family when they were children. Listening to these non-convergent stories, I realised that memories are inevitably perceptions of events rather than fact. Although the foundation of this book rests on factual findings, in as much as it also contains memories, it too is a blend of fact and fiction.

To bring life to the book and to help flesh out something of the times, places, personalities and interests of those long gone, I sought out memorabilia, including photographs. My father and his sisters wrote down selected memories when they were in their 80s. Seeing their handwriting is interesting: my father's eccentric prose with scant regard for punctuation and his insertion of capital Rs in the middle of woRds still makes me smile. As well as writing down some of his recollections, my father also tape recorded some of his thoughts over a whisky or two in 1980, his deeply spoken soft Welsh/North Eastern voice summing up his mixed pedigree.

Amassing what I knew and what I had been given made me feel that humanity's existence is quite fragile. My treasure chest consisted only of stories that did not always match, a box of faded photographs, some letters, a few birth, marriage and death certificates, an old milking stool, a battered wooden army trunk that had been to South Africa and back, and a family bible in Welsh with some names handwritten in the front. Looking at these things, I tried to piece together something of my ancestors' lives and thought how little of the story of their lives remained. These very personal links with the past were gradually supplemented by the usual genealogical finds in local record offices: parish registers, church documents, copies of wills, more birth, marriage and death certificates and census returns.

The story I am about to relate tells of repeated journeys over several generations between diagonally opposite ends of the UK: South Wales and North East England. I cringe rather as I write 'journeys' especially when I think how the word is overused nowadays by being bandied about on TV talent shows and in celebrity biographies. Nevertheless, this story is actually about journeys in that each generation has found one of the Lewises moving from one end of the UK to the other. Were these comings and goings moves towards something or away from something? As I carried out the research for this book, I tried to discover which motive might have prevailed at any given time. I may not always have got it right. That, I have decided, is the nature of history: events interpreted later by those with a varying balance of knowledge and imagination.

Is there a gene that determines whether or not we move away or stay in one place? If there is a get-up-and-go gene then my father, Kenneth, was the only one of his generation who inherited it. If he did inherit it, then it came from his father and his father's father before him.

In the days before the internet brought records straight into our homes, my research was a holiday pastime. I made frequent visits to South Wales throughout the 70s and early 80s. In 1986, I moved to South Wales for work and it became easier to trace and track lines of enquiry.

My father's sister, Isabel, in Llanelli, was keen to find out more about our ancestors. At this stage, I should point out to the reader that throughout the book you will find Llanelli, in Carmarthenshire, spelled in two different ways: Llanelly and Llanelli. Both are correct in the context in which they are used. Llanelli is the Welsh spelling which is used today. The spelling Llanelly is an anglicised form which was used in government and official documents until 1965 and that version appears in the book when I quote from something from an earlier time.

Isabel and I travelled to various places in Carmarthenshire associated with our forebears. In particular we went to Abergwili, a place of her youth. Once there, she began to remember things she had not recalled simply sitting at home.

We began to look for three family graves that she knew were in the churchyard of Abergwili parish church. Isabel quickly found two of the three memorial stones. One was a stone vase placed on a kerbed grave covered in stone chippings. Close examination of the moss-covered vase revealed an inscription to the memory of Frank (William Francis)

Lewis, her much loved father and my paternal grandfather. Frank spoke Welsh but was not from Wales.

The second memorial stone marked a grave by the church porch. The inscription was in memory of John Thomas and Esther Thomas (née Lewis), Isabel's mother's parents and my great grandparents. Both were buried with three of their tiny children, all under the age of 16 months, one only four days old.

IN LOVING MEMORY OF
THE CHILDREN OF
JOHN and ESTHER THOMAS
White Ox Abergwili
FRANCIS DIED NOV 15 1872
Aged 1 year and 5 months
JOHN DIED AUG 10 1873
Aged 4 days
BENJ. LLOYD DIED JUNE 28
1875 Aged 8 months
IN YOUR INNOCENCE AND BEAUTY
WITH A LIFE AS PURE AS SNOW
YOU ARE NESTLED IN TH BOSOM
OF THE CHRIST WE LOVE AND KNOW

ALSO JOHN THOMAS THE ABOVE
NAMED WHO DIED FEB 16 1890
AGED 45 YEARS
ALSO OF ESTHER WIFE OF THE ABOVE
JOHN THOMAS DIED FEB 18 1911
AGED 73 YEARS
BLESSED ARE THE DEAD WHICH DIE IN THE LORD

Kenneth and his sisters said that John and Esther had seven children. What misery to be pregnant year after year only to see your infants die. Young Francis died of scarlet fever. Babies John and Benjamin Lloyd died of convulsions. I never found where the other three were buried. Perhaps they were stillborn or miscarried, but the seventh child, Mary Valentine Thomas, my grandmother and later wife of William Francis (Frank) Lewis was the only one who survived to adulthood.

We did not find the oldest of the three graves. However, after a bit of a search we did find the memorial stone, unceremoniously dumped by a compost heap at the rear of the church. This stone was dedicated to the memory of William Lewis and Mary Lewis (née Francis), father and mother of Francis Lewis and the Esther Thomas (née Lewis) noted above. William and Mary were two of my great great grandparents.

SACRED
To the memory of Mary Lewis
The beloved wife of William
Lewis Late of Penygraig in this
Parish who died on the 26th of July
1849 aged 49 years
Also THOMAS LEWIS son of the
above named who died July 3rd
1854 aged 28 years
Also the Above William
Lewis who died August 4th
1874 aged 82 years

Within the space of ten or so metres, I had found the remains of three generations of ancestors, one of whom had been born in the late 1700s. At that moment I could not have told you anything about the 1700s. My school history stopped around the Stuarts and then there was a gap up to the second Elizabethan age.

As I looked at the stones in front of me, I tried to conjure up something to which I could relate. It slowly dawned on me that Esther was both Frank Lewis' aunt, and later in life, his mother-in law. Francis Lewis (Frank's father) and Esther Lewis (Frank's aunt and later mother-in-law) were brother and sister. The knowledge that Frank had married his first cousin shocked me rather. No offence meant, but I could not imagine marrying any of my cousins!

The dates and relationships on the three memorial stones set me off to look for more information in record offices and libraries. Before long I could have written an Egon Ronay-type guide to the ambience of record offices and the civility and helpfulness of archivists in various places in the North East of England and South Wales.

I visited the National Library of Wales in all its white stone splendour, perched high above the sea in Aberystwyth. It held the parish registers and wills that I needed from Carmarthenshire where I had found my forebears. The silent shelves and dusty tomes revealed a lot. I quickly found the baptismal dates of my great grandfather Francis Lewis and his nine brothers and sisters. I also discovered something about Francis' father,

William Lewis, my great great grandfather. There in the parish registers he is named as the reputed father of twin girls (Jane and Elizabeth) to someone described as Hannah, woman of Common, spinster. Common, I should add, was an area of Abergwili. And, if this was not enough local colour, a great great great great grandfather (Thomas Newall), described as a gentleman farmer, showed that he had enjoyed more than just an employer-employee relationship with his dairymaid (Mary Sampson). Thomas declared in his will that he was the father of the dairymaid's daughter, also Mary.

Back at home, I shared what I had found with my father and his sisters. If they knew anything of these tales they were giving little away. By now, I was intrigued to find out more about Francis Lewis. The fascination came from something I could not find rather than something I had found. I had discovered his baptismal details so I knew he was baptised in 1829. I also knew he lived with his family in 1841, but thereafter he seemed to slip out of the family altogether. There was no sign of him marrying in the area, nor could I find details of his death or burial. The fact that he was not known by his grandchildren, my father and his sisters, made me all the more curious.

Prepared by the experience of local record offices, and some information from my grandfather's birth certificate, I braced myself for a visit to London. Here I trawled through weighty volumes of birth, marriage and death certificate indexes in the central registry which at that time was in St Catherine's House. For each year, I combed through the quarterly volumes, each about two feet tall and around four inches thick. I searched for the marriage and the death of anyone by the name of Francis Lewis. I searched from the beginning of civil registration (September quarter of 1837) to a date by which I knew he was dead. My paternal grandfather's marriage certificate in 1901 described his father (Francis) as deceased. To find the death certificate reference alone meant lifting and sifting through 254 volumes. All the while I was looking for someone whose age at the time of death matched a person who was born around 1829.

The result of many hours' weight training was the discovery that only one person had details that matched a Francis Lewis of the right sort of age in the marriage and death indexes. This Francis Lewis had married

Isabella Bird in 1860 in Escomb, County Durham. Later, in 1881, he had died in Stockton-on-Tees nearly 300 miles away from his birthplace.

My father knew nothing of his grandfather, nor why he had gone to the North East, nor how he had arrived there so long ago. It was to be my task to find out.

The early Welsh Lewises: farmers, drovers and publicans

When and why did Francis Lewis leave rural Carmarthenshire in South Wales? I knew he had left sometime between 1841 and 1860. It was to take nearly 30 years and the electronic release of the 1851 census before I was able to track him down more closely.

In the meantime, I wondered why he had gone to County Durham and how he had made the journey in the 1800s which even today can take the best part of 10 hours by car. For years, I dipped in and out of records in the hope of finding out what I wanted to know. Francis Lewis did not give up his life story very easily. As I probed records and lines of enquiry, I added a lot to the stories of Francis' parents, his grandparents and great grandparents. Without knowing something of them, it is difficult to understand Francis and his descendants. So I shall fill you in a little on my ancestor's ancestors. You can have a look for yourself at the end of the book where I have included some extracts from my family tree.

Francis was descended, probably going back hundreds of years, from farmers in the beautiful county of Carmarthenshire. The Lewis family has its origins in a few quiet villages along and above the Towy valley to the east of Carmarthen town.

My search backwards from Francis came to an impasse with the baptism of his grandfather, John Lewis. There are two John Lewises shown as the likely ones on the same page of the Llanfynydd baptismal records in 1765. One is John son of William David Lewis and the other is John son of Thomas Lewis.

I am inclined to think 'our' John is the son of William David, only because the name William crops up over and over in several generations of Lewises. David also crops up a few times, whereas Thomas comes up less often. But, in truth, I do not know if this would be a correct assumption.

All I know is that John Lewis was born in 1765 during the long reign of King George III, in the tiny village of Llanfynydd which nestles near the Black Mountains north east of Carmarthen. He was the son of a farmer and he was my great great great grandfather.

John Lewis married Mary Newall by licence in the parish church in Llanarthney in 1788. Both parties were literate as they signed their names in the register. One of the witnesses was Thomas Newall, Mary's father and another was Sarah Lewis, possibly John's sister. Thomas Newall is an interesting character of whom we shall soon learn more.

Around the turn of the 18th century, John Lewis, by then a farmer himself, became a prominent and respected figure in the nearby village of Llanarthney in the Towy Valley. John's name and signature appear over twenty years in many Llanarthney parish records as an overseer of the poor and as a churchwarden. The local farmers and gentlemen landowners ran their communities much as councils might do nowadays, electing officers from amongst their midst, making up and enforcing rules and deciding on rates, rights and responsibilities.

John lived on a couple of different farms, Llwyn du (in Welsh – Black or Dark Grove) and Plas uchaf (High Place), a mile or so to the south of Llanarthney.

This photograph of Llwyn du was taken in the 1980s. If you remove the pneumatic tyre and maybe the Old English sheepdog in the yard, I doubt that it would have looked too much different in the 1800s.

He appears to have come by these properties from his father-in-law, Thomas Newall, rather than from his own father. Presumably John left some of the farming to others as the records show that his life seemed to revolve around the church and parish meetings.

With other gentlemen of the parish, John Lewis busied himself in vestry meetings during which he and his fellow churchmen set the rate (seven shillings and sixpence in the pound in 1805) that occupiers of land, tenements and woods had to pay each year to assist the poor. That same year, they assessed the sum for the maintenance of the church and churchyard at two pence in the pound. They handed out to the poor of the parish either cash or clothes and other goods as they deemed fit. Men and women with no other means of support were granted money at the vestry meetings, or perhaps a new shirt, a dress or a pair of wooden shoes. All of these expenses were carefully recorded for posterity in the vestry books.

On 24 October 1806, the elected few in Llanarthney, including John Lewis churchwarden, showed significant social leadership by agreeing to enter into a capital project to help educate the youngsters of the village. They drew up a plan to build a schoolhouse. I wonder what he would have thought if he had known that so many of his descendants would later become schoolteachers. With very little effort, I can think of at least eight in the family who went into that calling over 160 years later.

John and his colleagues decided on and recorded the exact dimensions and materials to be used to erect the community asset. The details recorded in the parish books were effectively an architect's specification:

'...side walls to be 20 inches thick by 15 foot high of good stones and mortar...5 windows 2 of them 4 foot by 3...3 upstairs to be one pane shorter in hight...rafters 3 inches by 2½ all of the above timber to be of hart of oak...glasing and painting in good workmanlike maner and plastering inside...'

All of the building was to be completed for the sum of £60 by 3 February 1807, half to be paid on 1 January 1807 and the other half on completing the job, '...in the time and manor and from as afore said mentiond... or they shall forfeit one moiety or half payment...'. There was no let out clause for poor weather getting in the way, which it might well have done starting the project as they did in the run up to winter.

On 6 April 1821, in the first year of the reign of King George IV, John Lewis of Plas uchaf, in his role as an overseer of the poor, agreed with one John Jones to award money at a weekly rate to keep a certain Lettice Bowler until Michaelmas 1821. At the same meeting, he agreed that Mary Zachariah should have a new shift (dress). During that meeting, it is also recorded that every overseer of the poor (four local gentlemen) should raise the sum of £20 each for the space of three calendar months to pay for the relief of the poor for whom they were responsible.

Another obligation that fell to these elected parish men was that they were the named persons to whom reputed fathers of illegitimate children were bound in the form of bastardy orders. These orders ensured that the financial needs of children born outside of marriage were met by those who had fathered them so that the children did not become a burden on parish relief. The orders stated the sum of money that the reputed fathers had to set by for the education and maintenance of their illegitimately born children, usually until the children were old enough to be apprenticed (14 years of age) or put to work.

The whole issue of who fathered children was very much open to the community. No super injunctions keeping things quiet in those days! The names of reputed fathers were there for all to see in parish registers and other records. Indeed, John's own wife, Mary Newall, was known to be the reputed daughter of another gentleman, Thomas Newall, who was never married to Mary's mother, Mary Sampson. I do not think that Thomas was Welsh and I have so far not found any trace of his origins. His surname seems to be most prominent in the North West of England and the North West lowlands of Scotland. Thomas remains a challenge for another time.

Ironically, gentleman Newall is a signatory to several bastardy orders made against other men in the village. Thomas Newall seems to have needed no such pressing as he acknowledges, in his very detailed will, the fact that Mary Newall was his daughter by his illiterate dairymaid, Mary Sampson. Thomas was a bachelor living in Llwyn du, a house on the Middleton estate where the National Botanic Garden of Wales was established. Whether or not he would have been so keen to acknowledge his child had he been married to someone else, who knows?

In 1798, the French were threatening to invade Britain during the

Napoleonic wars. Indeed they had already landed briefly in Wales the year before. But Thomas Newall was busy with more immediate things: drawing up his will of which John Lewis was sole executor. He left £50 and many of his worldly goods to Mary Sampson for the duration of her life. The worldly goods being, '...*one feather bed, bedstead and appurtenances, one square table, six chairs, one cupboard, twelve pewter plates, half a dozen knives and forks, one iron pot, one iron kettle, and one bakestone...*'. He even left William Sampson (Mary Sampson's father) the sum of six guineas. Thomas also tried to ensure that Mary Sampson passed on her worldly goods through her will in accordance with his wishes. He wrote into his own will that when his dairymaid died, the bulk of her estate should go to one of the sons of John Lewis and Mary Newall his wife, a boy tactfully named Thomas after his grandfather. The other children of John and Mary fared less well, although the second son, William Lewis (my great grandfather) was lucky enough to receive Thomas Newall's *'best desk'*. However, not wishing him to be profligate with his new-found property, the desk was to be held in trust until William reached the age of discretion.

Thomas Newall went on to state that money accrued from interest on various properties should go equally to all John and Mary's children for their education and for their more general benefit once they reached the age of 21. Thomas Newall died in Llanarthney in 1799. John Lewis as executor, received for his trouble a sort of, 'anything-I-have-not-already-mentioned', kind of bequest, as '...*all my stock, crop, goods, chattels and personals of what kind or nature so ever they consist or wheresoever to be found; not above bequeathed or specified, subject to the payment of all my just debts...*'.

Mary Sampson made her will six years later. At that time it was unusual for women to make wills as until 1870 married women were not allowed officially to own any property. In the event, Mary was single and did not quite follow Thomas' instructions. With John Lewis as executor once again, she determined that he should share out to all her grandchildren, apart from William, the money and goods, passed to her by Thomas Newall. The will shows the same feather bed, pewter plates, knives and forks etc. being passed on to the eldest child of John and Mary Lewis' children, Mary, who also inherited her clothes, a chest and a box. The other children with the exception of William each received £10 to be held in trust until they reached the age of *'one and twenty'*. Quite what William's offence had been to be so ignored, we shall never know. John Lewis as executor received the interest accruing from her money for his trouble.

John Lewis died in Plas uchaf on 4 March 1826 aged 61. John appears to have died without having left a will. His wife, Mary, was later granted letters of administration on the understanding that his estate did not amount to more than £200. This sum of £200 does not sound much nowadays, but it would have been six or seven times what an agricultural labourer at that time might have earned in a year.

The impression I have of John is of someone who spent a lot of time in the service of his community: an earnest man trusted by his father-in-law and mother-in-law to be the executor of their respective wills. Although Thomas Lewis, John and Mary's son was a principal inheritor of the wealth of Thomas Newall, I could not track him down in any of the property left by Thomas Newall in his will. I think, perhaps, he died between 1799 when Thomas Newall left him so much in his will and 1806 when Mary Sampson fails to mention him in her will. One of the younger brothers, John Lewis and his wife, also a Mary, farmed at Plas uchaf for many years.

John Lewis senior's second son, William Lewis, my great great grandfather, was born in the 1790s in Llanarthney, Carmarthenshire. William was not a great landowner but a yeoman farmer for over 20 years. He farmed at Pen-y-graig, in the hamlet of Cricklas near Abergwili, a village some seven miles to the west of Llanarthney.

The impression I have of William is one quite different from his father. William was living in Pen-y-graig in 1817 as a bachelor when he was exposed in parish registers as the father of twin girls to Hannah of Common in the parish register. Three years later William married not Hannah but Mary Francis. Mary was a daughter of a major Carmarthenshire landowner from Llangathen, another village along the Towy Valley. Judging by Mary Francis' parents' standing and her brothers' land holdings in various farms around Carmarthenshire, she appears to have married a little beneath her by taking William as her husband.

William and Mary had nine children in the course of the next twenty years, at least one of whom died in childhood. All but the last two were born at the farm, Pen-y-graig near Abergwili. By the 1840s, the Lewis family fortunes had changed. William and Mary had lost or given up the farm and William was no longer a farmer. Pen-y-graig was by then occupied by Mary's brother William Francis and his family. William Lewis' eldest son John, aged 15, was living with the Francis family in an outbuilding of Pen-y-graig.

Pen-y-graig in the 1980s

Although he had no recollection just which generation was involved, my father, Kenneth, remembered family tales about the loss of a farm with lawyers called in to sort out the situation. Kenneth's scepticism of lawyers probably came from hearing that the only persons to receive benefit after it was all over were the lawyers themselves. Locals in the area only remembered the farm as belonging to the Francis family, so perhaps the Francises had rented it out to William Lewis only to take it back at some stage.

William left the farm in the late 1830s when there had been two very poor harvests. South West Wales suffered from seasons of very heavy rainfall which forced farmers to buy corn at famine prices to simply feed their families and their animals. Then, in the 1840s, the repeal of the Corn Laws added to the burden of hard-pressed farmers, driving many from the land or into service employment.

By 1841, William Lewis had moved into Abergwili village and was turning his hand to being a publican living at the Farmers' Arms in Abergwili. He lived there with his wife Mary and three of their sons, William, Francis and James. The Farmers' Arms is no longer there but in 1841 it was positioned neatly and somewhat incongruously between the Bishop's Palace and a pauper's house. A year later when his last child was born, William was also a toll keeper. Given the distaste with which tolls were viewed in Wales, William was clearly his own man.

In 1849, Mary Lewis, aged 49, was one of the thousands who died from the dreadful scourge of typhus, a bacterial disease carried by lice, fleas and rats. People caught typhus when the lice and fleas that had bitten their host then defecated on the skin. The human host would scratch the bite and once the skin was broken through scratching, the deadly bacterium carried in the flea faeces entered the body. Typhus was a virulent disease that was responsible for killing hundreds of thousands of French soldiers in the Napoleonic wars in the early 1800s, more than were killed by the Russians.

Thankfully, many of the bacterial diseases that were so deadly in the 19th century have been all but eradicated from our lives in the west, or else they are treatable with antibiotics. But, in the 19th century, once a disease like typhus took hold it meant almost certain doom. Until I studied microbiology, my only knowledge of this disease came from seeing the film Dr Zhivago and recalling Omar Sharif's made-up grey complexion and hacking cough. The actual symptoms of typhus are much worse than any make-up artist achieved with Omar Sharif. The person would suffer fever, headache, weakness, muscle aches and a rash composed of both spots and bumps. The rash would start on the back, chest and abdomen then spread to the arms and legs. The worst types of complications would be hidden from view, involving swelling in the heart muscle or brain.

Typhus was known in Britain in the 1840s as the 'Irish fever'. It had reached epidemic proportions in Ireland in 1846 to 1849 during the Great Famine. It spread from Ireland to mainland Britain by some of the vast numbers of Irish who fled their country in search of food and work. Once the disease reached all parts of the mainland, it flared up in serious outbreaks, often in conjunction with other diseases like influenza, cholera and dysentery.

Tens of thousands of those unlucky enough to be in its way were wiped out.

As publicans, William and Mary would have been exposed more than most to infections brought by travellers thirsting for refreshments and looking for lodgings as they passed through the village. Abergwili had a lot of visitors in that period as it was a place where cattle fairs were held. With the coming of the railway around the 1840s and 50s, visitor numbers were swelled, further contributing to the spread of disease.

The 1840s were particularly bad times for the poor of the land. Food was scarce and prices were high. The poor were underfed and had little resistance to disease. Life expectancy for men and women in the 1840s was 40 and 42 respectively. For labourers, mechanics and servants, life was even shorter but by no means sweet, with the average age at death being only fifteen.

In the early part of the long reign of Queen Victoria, diseases including influenza, typhoid, cholera and typhus were endemic, products of poor sanitation and overcrowded living. In Wales around this time, for example, cholera spread from Cardiff up to Merthyr Tydfil, Dowlais and Aberdare, killing 800.

People's knowledge of disease and its causes was limited and few properly understood the link between hygiene and health. Even if they had understood, doing something about it would have been difficult. During the first decades of Victoria's reign, baths were virtually unknown in the poorer districts and uncommon anywhere. Most households of all economic classes still used privy-pails; water closets were rare.

Privy pails were simply buckets enclosed beneath wooden boards with holes that acted as seats. As many as a hundred individuals in a town might use a communal privy into which all their liquid and solid waste would go. Ashes from the fire were tipped onto the pails to help absorb some of the liquid and dampen down the smell of the contents in between times when the pails were carted away at night to be emptied.

Even in the late 1950s and early 1960s, I can remember going to visit distant cousins of my father in Abergwili and having to visit the privy down the garden. At the height of summer it stank and buzzed with flies. As a 9 year old, it was something I had not experienced. I was shocked to think that people lived like that.

In 1851, a couple of years after his wife's death, William was living with Esther the elder of his two daughters in Abergwili. He was still a victualler and father and daughter lived in the public house. Three of his sons, John (26), Thomas (23) and James (10) were living and working with their unmarried uncle and aunt, John and Sarah Francis. John and Sarah had a 210 acre farm, Pentre Davis, in Llangathen. This place is a rural idyll along the edge of the Towy valley overlooking Golden Grove and near to the recently restored Aberglasney gardens. There was no sign of Francis who by now would have been 22.

In 1854, William's son Thomas Lewis died. He had moved with John and Sarah Francis from Pentre Davis to a farm known as Rogerlay just outside Kidwelly in the south of Carmarthenshire. The influence of the industrial revolution was showing as at the time of his death he was working in a tin mill rather than on the farm. Thomas' death certificate says he died of arachnitis. When I first read that, I thought he must have had some terrible encounter with a spider but then found out that arachnitis is inflammation of the arachnoid membrane surrounding the brain and spinal cord. His death certificate might have recorded meningitis if it was today.

At the time of the census in 1861, William, Esther and James were staying with William's brother-in-law and sister-in-law, the John and Sarah Francis I have already mentioned. So, William's relationship with his deceased wife's family seemed to have remained a cordial one. John and Sarah Francis were living on another of their farms, the smaller but still substantive 86 acre Rogerlay.

By the time of the 1871 census, William was back in Abergwili in another public house, the White Ox. This is now number 6 High Street, Abergwili. William lived here with Esther, his eldest daughter, by then married, and her husband John Thomas, a former slate quarryman. I can't help but feel that the name William chose for his public house was a cheeky jibe at the still standing Black Ox further along the High Street in the village.

Either he was very fit, or his sense of humour showed again as William described himself in the 1871 census as a cattle drover, aged 74, understating his age by some degree.

Cattle were major exports from Wales to England before the coming of the coal and iron industries. One of the cattle droving routes from West Wales turned northwards at Abergwili before leading on to Lampeter and then to the English border and Hereford. There were two fairs held each year in Abergwili, later increasing to three with the coming of the railway. Many cattle were bought in Abergwili and then driven into England at the rate of a couple of miles an hour. I can imagine William accompanying the Welsh black cattle over the hills of Carmarthenshire stopping at hostelries en route enjoying the fruits of his labour and many a yarn before coming back home to Abergwili. This is a man who was prepared to be a poacher turned gamekeeper being at times both a drover and a toll keeper. It was said that drovers would rather lose a day by making a long detour than pay to go through a gate with their stock.

William died at the White Ox in 1874. He was in his 80s – nearly twice the age he might have expected to live at this time. He died from heart disease and dropsy, an old medical term for swelling of the feet and lower legs. Nowadays, he might have been recorded as having died from congestive heart disease, as one of his great granddaughters did some 80 years later.

William seems to have been a man who loved life and lived life. He comes off the page as a big character, full of bonhomie sitting in a public house drinking and exchanging stories. He was bilingual. Although Welsh would have been his day-to-day language at home and in his work, he probably did not write Welsh but both he and his father John were able to read English and Welsh and write English in a neat and confident hand.

Not surprisingly, William did not leave much behind materially. On 26 September 1877, three years after his death, the administration of his effects was granted to his daughter, Esther. His effects were valued at under £40 (an equivalent spending power nowadays of just under £2,000).

As the photograph following shows, after the death of her father and later her husband in 1890, Esther became licensee of the White Ox. Esther Thomas is the figure in the doorway. She was widowed in her early 50s and, rather like Queen Victoria after the death of Prince Albert, wore black clothes (widow's weeds) for the rest of her life. Her young daughter Mary is seated by the window in front of the public house. The photograph must have been taken in the 1890s and the baby on her knee probably belonged to a neighbour.

The White Ox was a basic watering hole for local farmers and itinerant workers. The beer was supplied by Buckley's in Llanelli. This brewery had been established rather surprisingly by a Methodist, Henry Child. A Methodist minister, the Reverend James Buckley, married Henry Child's daughter, Maria, and went on to develop the brewery.

Beer was kept in small casks or firkins which stood on thick slate slabs. In summer, the casks were covered by wet sacks to keep them cool. The casks were tapped with brass taps and serving the beer to ensure that no hops got into the drink was a skilled art. Drink was served from jugs into individually-owned pots kept behind the bar by thirsty regulars. The bar was essentially the front room of what was otherwise a house. Welsh was the language of choice on a day-to-day basis in the bar room and in the home. Mrs Thomas was a strict churchwoman and the place was run according to her rules: no swearing or bad language and no rowdy behaviour.

My father recalled tales of the place from his early childhood. Telling the following anecdote gives a flavour of Esther as licensee and the rough characters who no doubt frequented the place.

A group of men came in for their usual refreshments but unusually they were given their drinks in stony silence by the landlady.

One of the men said, in Welsh, 'There's quiet you are Mrs Thomas. Aren't you speaking to me?'

She looked back and said she was not happy with his behaviour when he was in the day before.

The man scratched his head and replied, 'What did I do or say Mrs Thomas?'

Esther replied, 'You told me to go to hell!'

The room quietened as they waited for the man's apology but instead he looked at her, winked and said, 'God, there's quick you've come back!'

The leaving of the land

Francis, William and Mary's fourth son was given his mother's maiden name as his Christian name when he was baptised in Abergwili Parish Church in the spring of 1829. That same year, as the reign of King George IV drew to a close, was a time when people were migrating in their thousands from a life on the land to emerging industries and urban developments.

Francis was clearly not destined to remain at home and be a publican: that was work for women and old men. Unlike his brothers, he did not stay with the lush green land of Carmarthenshire and the bucolic life of the farm. Francis probably left home in the late 1840s or early 1850s once he had reached the age of majority. The family no longer had a farm which might have employed him and the death of his mother in the heat of the summer of 1849 would have done nothing to keep him in Abergwili. It took me years to find out where Francis first went on leaving Abergwili. I had nothing to give me any clue so had to wait until the 1851 census was released and searchable online. When that day came, I finally found Francis still in Wales but some 60 miles away in a very different place from Abergwili and the Towy Valley.

As the railways spread their iron arteries across South Wales, Francis had left his rural life, taken the train and travelled east to the town of Merthyr Tydfil, the centre of the iron industry. He had left the land in favour of the excitement and noise that was pulling men and women from the country towards towns and cities as the industrial revolution took hold.

The Merthyr Tydfil of the early 1800s was the Welsh boom town without equal, an exciting place hugely swelling its numbers with young, able-bodied men and some women from all over Wales. Its population had grown from a town of nearly 8,000 in 1801 to an industrial place of over 43,000 by 1851. Most of its inhabitants in the 1850s were young and 80% were Welsh, mainly drawn from the rural parts of South and West

Wales. Alongside the Welsh-speaking majority was a growing number of Irish who had steadily been crossing the Irish Sea in search of better prospects since the potato famine of the 1840s.

But Merthyr had the same problem that all emerging towns and cities had in the 19th century. It did not have the infrastructure to cope properly with the influx of so many people that, in the 1840s and 1850s, made it the largest town in Wales. Contemporary writers spoke of the terrible working and living conditions which were poor at best and generally appalling.

The town's air was filthy with soot and at night the skies were ablaze from the continuously burning furnaces. Little wonder that in 1850 when Thomas Carlyle the satirist, essayist and historian visited Merthyr Tydfil he described it as, '...*the squalidest, ugliest place on earth*', and '...*his vision of hell*'.

By the late 1840s, Merthyr Tydfil had the highest death rate in Wales and one of the highest in the whole of Britain. Diseases spread quickly because of the living conditions. The supply of fresh water to the inhabitants of Merthyr was very poor. Sewers had flat bottoms, and because drains were made out of stone, seepage could be considerable. Streets were often unpaved and, especially after rain, the streets might remain ankle-deep in disease-holding mud for weeks.

The River Taff ran through the town but it was diverted for use in the ironworks and was akin to an open sewer. It was a key source of life-threatening diseases like cholera and typhoid. Over a hundred people might share a privy or cess-pit that stank and in summer was infested with disease-carrying flies. Similar numbers might queue for water from one pump, water that was often contaminated with sewage and animal waste.

The iron company owners imposed a penny a week charge on each of their houses to pay for the collection and disposal of household refuse. Refuse of all kinds was simply thrown into the streets for collection and caused an obstruction for the very carts sent to pick it up. When the refuse was removed, it was taken to a tip on the north side of Dowlais where it was left to rot causing more danger to those living nearby.

The Health of Towns Commission investigated the state of Merthyr in 1844, and Sir Henry de la Beche, reporting on the drainage and sanitation of the town, wrote:

'In these respects the town is in a sad state of neglect; with the exception of some little care in the main streets and regulations about removing ashes before the doors in Dowlais, all else is in a miserable condition. From the poorer inhabitants, who constitute the mass of the population, throwing all slops and refuse into the nearest open gutter before their houses, from the impeded course of such channels and the scarcity of privies, some parts of the town are complete networks of filth, emitting noxious exhaltations (sic). Fortunately the fall of the ground is commonly so good that heavy rains carry away some of this filth. There is no Local Act for drainage and cleansing, the Highway Act being that in force, and the chief lines of road appearing to be under the Commissioners of the Turnpikes. During the rapid increase of this town no attention seems to have been paid to its drainage and the streets and houses have been built at random, as it suited the views of those who speculated in them.'

The chairman of the Board of Guardians in Merthyr, together with two surgeons and an attorney, testified to the accuracy of the Commissioner's Report, adding that:

'... the few public sewers were cleansed by rain-water only' and that *'such a thing as a house drain was never heard of here'.*

While the iron masters sank their own private wells, water spouts and springs were the chief sources of water for the majority of the population. However, these spouts and springs were subject to the vagaries of the rainfall in the area. During the summer many dried up and most were intermittently fed by surface water undoubtedly heavily contaminated by household refuse. Many people would resort to using the river and canals for washing but it was not unusual to see people relieving themselves in these places whilst yards away, others would be filling pitchers for domestic use.

For years, the iron masters resisted the construction of a proper reservoir higher up the valley. As far as they were concerned the importance of water power to the industry was far more significant than the problems caused by the shortage of a decent domestic supply of water to their workers. Life was cheap, infrastructure was expensive.

Yet despite the working and living conditions, people kept coming to take their chance amongst the furnaces and rolling mills. They put up with the terrible conditions because young able-bodied men from small rural communities could earn three times as much as the shilling a day they might have received as a farm servant or agricultural labourer.

Francis moved from Abergwili to Merthyr Tydfil at a very inauspicious time. The iron industry was going through one of its frequent, although not always long-lasting, slumps. Between 1847 and 1850, wages were cut by 40% and redundancies were becoming more and more common. Men made redundant could not expect to receive parish relief. The parish was straining to cope with those who were ill or infirm, or those whose circumstances left them unable to work. Those who were made redundant were usually unskilled labourers. They were expected to move on elsewhere to look for work or return to the farms from whence they had come. But the slump of the late 1840s and early 1850s was different as even skilled men became redundant and they had to leave and look elsewhere for work. Work only picked up again in 1854 when iron was needed for armaments for the Crimean War.

Merthyr Tydfil struggled to cope with housing, the influx of people, and dealing with the high birth rate that resulted from young people pouring into the town without parental control. Alongside the high birth rate, there was also an appallingly high death rate, with children under the age of five accounting for over half of the deaths in the town.

Crime too was a great issue. In the late 1840s, there were nineteen policemen, roughly one per 2,000 people to deal with offences caused within the burgeoning town. A Chief Constable of the time was convinced that there was a positive correlation between larceny and the level of unemployment arising from the fluctuating state of the iron industry.

Poverty accounted for some crimes, such as the theft of clothing and food. The iron works themselves were the centre of other crimes such as thefts of coal, damage to property and illegal strikes. Stealing coal from the iron works accounted for a large proportion of all cases heard at the court sessions. Colliers' wives were known to put stones on the tracks of railroads to cause the trucks to shake and drop off coals. Waiting children then picked up the coal and made off with it in baskets.

What might be called leisure crimes like drunkenness, violence and disorderly behaviour also put a strain on policing. The evenings following pay days were times when men were seen reeling and staggering about the streets after frittering away their cash in the local hostelries. Some staggered home while others delayed their home-going by fighting in the streets.

Whilst drunkenness and violence were mainly the provinces of young males, women were also known to cause mayhem after drinking too much. Some notables, who went by the gloriously descriptive names of 'Snuffy Nell' Sullivan and 'Saucy Stack' Edwards, were well known to the police in that regard, as was Julia Carroll, 'the heroine of a hundred brawls'.

Crimes of a sexual or family-related nature, such as rape, indecent assault, incest, infanticide and so on were known but often not reported. The authorities mainly focussed on crimes obliquely associated with sex, namely theft whilst in the company of prostitutes. This crime was particularly frequent in an area of Merthyr Tydfil that became known as 'China' or the 'empire'.

In 'China', forty to sixty prostitutes worked to separate their clients from their money in one way or another. This 'empire' was ruled by an 'emperor' and 'empress', both of whom were eventually transported for their sins, only to be succeeded by a new 'imperial' regime. It was a well-established routine to steal from the person ill-advised enough to go to this area to seek his pleasures as soon as he became too drunk or too compromised to notice what was happening. Women well known for their strength with names like, 'Big Jane', 'The Buffalo' and 'Big Nell' did the necessary to assist the 'nymphs' or prostitutes to part the client from his money. If extra help was needed men known as 'Bullies' stood by to give a hand.

The response of the courts to crime varied greatly. They could be very tough indeed as shown by the case of a 14 year old boy who, with previous convictions, was transported for 10 years for stealing one and a half loaves of bread. However, many cases of theft from the ironworks were dismissed by magistrates as being the fault of the iron masters themselves for failing to secure their property, i.e. culpable negligence. The rural magistrates from the wider Glamorgan area had little sympathy with the iron masters. Many felt the latter had ignored the traditional relationships between masters and their workforce, had robbed the agricultural estates of much-needed labour and created communities of immoral people given to argument and disorder.

So it was, in this environment, in 1851, aged 21 and single, that Francis had become an iron miner for the Dowlais Iron Company. The company had been founded in 1759 by nine individuals who built a furnace to produce iron. In its first year, the primitive furnace had produced 500 tons of iron. As time went on, more land was leased and more furnaces were built along with mills, forges and housing for the workers. By 1767, John Guest of Shropshire was appointed manager and later he became a partner. By 1842, over 5,000 people were employed in the company in seventeen blast furnaces. Just three years later in 1845, Dowlais Ironworks, still in the ownership of the Guest family, was the biggest ironworks in the world. With 8,800 employees, it produced 88,400 tons yearly from 18 blast furnaces.

Over a third of the workers in Merthyr Tydfil were miners and colliers. Some mines were inclines driven into the hillsides surrounding the town while others were accessed by shafts. Sometimes miners looking for iron and colliers looking for coal worked at different levels in the same mine while other mines were exclusively for either iron or coal.

The mining was done using a 'post and stall' method where areas or 'stalls' were mined and vertical areas or 'posts' of stone were left untouched to hold up the roof and stabilise the surroundings. Both miners and colliers worked in cramped, often wet and dangerous conditions and were exposed to constant dust and extremes of temperatures. A local newspaper reported in 1850 that the job of the miner was harder than that of the collier. However, the pay of the miner was lower as the collier was given extra pay to compensate for the threat of explosions from fire damp.

Dressed in a flannel shirt, fustian (a cheap cotton-linen mix) trousers and with handkerchiefs tied tightly around his head, Francis would have used a hammer and large iron chisel to bore a hole a few feet into the rock at an upward angle. Into the hole, he would have placed a cartridge of strong gunpowder sealed in place by a clay plug containing a fuse. He would be careful how he used these cartridges, not least because he had to pay for them himself. After lighting the fuse, Francis would have retreated quickly to a safe distance to await the explosion that he would hope would reveal a vein of ironstone. Using a crowbar and wedges he would then have broken down the ironstone seam and loaded it into trams for it to be carried away in a small truck (a dram) for weighing.

Iron miners were paid by the ton of ironstone that they extracted. Each dram containing their spoils would bear a metal tag to show whose work it was and the tallying would be done at the surface. The amount paid would fluctuate a lot depending on both demand and the accessibility of the stone. The workers underground had no control over the recording of their output and accusations of false weighing were frequent and often led to heated arguments and fights.

A system of long pay existed. In other words, it was often six or seven weeks before employees were paid in full although in Dowlais the workers could draw down some of their pay as 'subs' each week. The iron masters made out that weekly pay was not possible because of the shortage of coins and the fact that so many workers were paid by measure of weight of mineral extracted or distance of mine excavated. However, they also thought that regular payments at the end of each week would lead to more absenteeism the following Monday.

Wages were affected by stoppages designed to support the workers, to encourage good behaviour and to discourage unreliability. By the 1840s, all the works in Merthyr Tydfil had established medical schemes to provide doctors, medicine and sick pay if the worker was ill or injured. In 1850, in Dowlais, the charge was 3 farthings (three quarters of an old penny) a week. Other 'benefits' paid for by stoppages included the provision of housing, schooling, coal and the replenishment of tools, candles and gunpowder. The Dowlais Company tackled absenteeism especially that which incurred after a weekend of heavy drinking by giving workers a bonus of one or two pence a ton for their iron if they worked regularly. The workers were also fined if they took time off for no good cause and they were taken to court if their absenteeism was excessive.

Working underground with the miners were many others including cutters who made new roadways into the mine and hauliers who, with large strong horses, carted off the spoils of the mining.

The hours worked were long, twelve to thirteen hours a day for six days a week. If the worker was trying to boost his production and hence his pay as pay day approached, he might put in eighteen-hour shifts. Miners took food down the mine with them – usually bread and cheese and closed tin jugs of cold tea, milk or water. They ate their food whenever it was convenient, hunkering down as a change of position within their cramped surroundings.

Only two days were recognised as holidays, Good Friday and Christmas Day. It was not until the 1860s that the half-day Saturday movement threatened to change the old order. The ironmasters argued strongly against any change to the existing arrangements saying that the men had too much time off as it was because of accidents and absenteeism.

Not only men worked in the ironworks. Women made bricks for the kilns and furnaces and stacked coal for coking prior to it being tipped into the furnaces. These women would have to lift large weights of coal, some individual pieces weighing over a hundredweight. It was filthy work in all weathers, rain, snow, frost and the heat of summer. Some women broke up limestone for the furnaces, smashing it into fragments with heavy hammers. Other women known as pilers, wearing no more special protective clothing than leather gloves, worked in pairs stacking iron bars ready for the balling furnaces. They shifted around 35 tons of often very hot metal a day between them. Near the furnaces, women known as pollers worked alongside men emptying iron ore from trucks, separating it from shale and piling it ready for the furnaces. Women as tip girls emptied cinders from the furnaces. Others operated winches and water balances that raised the iron ore and coal. The winch operators were amongst the best paid women at around £2 a month. The tip girls and the pollers were the least well paid at around 4 shillings for a seven day week.

Even children as young as seven worked around the mines often as air-door keepers who opened and closed the doors for the hauliers with their horses and trams. Teenage girls filled drams with coal or ironstone and dragged them along workings that were as low as 30 inches high. These young girls would make up to fifty or so journeys a day dragging four or five hundredweight of mineral by means of chains attached to their waists. In the course of a 12-hour shift, they were hauling loads of 10 or 11 tons. Furnace men employed boys as underhands in the hope that they would take on their own furnace by the time they were twenty. Some children were paid by the men they worked with while others were hired directly by the company. Hauliers in the mine in 1850 were paid 12 shillings (about 60p) a week while an air door opener was paid 2 shillings and 6 pence (about 12½p) a week. However, whether they were boys or girls, the money was given to their fathers, in the case of a boy until he was 17 or married, and in the case of a girl until she married. All the children could hope for was up to about 6 old pence (6d) as pocket money.

Francis boarded in a house in Mary Street, Dowlais with a total of seven occupants. The building, called a second-class house, was probably owned by the Dowlais Iron Company. Such a house might typically have had two small rooms, possibly three. It would have had small windows, stone floors, maybe with a rag mat and a black range-type coal fire. It would have had no toilet, sewer or running water. As for furniture, aside from beds which two or more might have had to share, perhaps in shifts, there might have been a table, chairs and a cupboard in the living room with the coal fire. For sanitation, the inhabitants used chamber pots which were emptied into the streets, or the river. It was common to see males relieving themselves, *'without the commonest regard for decency'*. A doctor from the Board of Health who visited in 1853 said that he had seen the worst parts of London, Manchester and Bristol but he *'...never did see anything which could compare with Merthyr...'*. The same doctor describes seeing a young woman filling her water pitcher from a little stream gushing from a cinder heap. He saw intestinal worms being washed into the water the woman was collecting. When schools were opened in Dowlais, the children had to be taught how to use the toilets.

Francis' landlady in Mary Street was Rachel Hughes, a 44 year old widow from Merthyr Tydfil who no doubt took in lodgers to provide an additional source of income. Despite the lack of proper washing and toilet facilities and the filth that surrounded them, she and other women in this area would have worked hard to keep the insides of their thinly-furnished houses clean and tidy.

Rachel had three sons aged 16, 13 and 5, the eldest two of whom worked in a coal mine as haulier and collier respectively. As well as Francis Lewis, she had also taken in two other boarders: John and Walter Williams from Llanelli in Carmarthenshire. These men were iron puddlers, a skilled job to which Francis probably aspired as it would have paid more money than his miner's wages. Five doors away lived John Lewis (no relation), an 11 year old door keeper in the colliery. In a back-to-back house in a nearby street, 9 year old Mary Samuel had already begun working as a stone breaker. Further along in New South Wales Street, were colliers John Morris and William Watts, aged 8 and 11 respectively. In the same street, David Price, aged 9, had already started his apprenticeship as a stone mason.

Mary Street and the surrounding streets in Dowlais were full of men and women from Glamorgan, Monmouthshire, Carmarthenshire and Pembrokeshire. They were virtually all iron workers and colliers toiling long and hard in hot and filthy conditions making the thousands of tons of iron that poured out of the furnaces and down the valleys by rail to ships in Cardiff and Newport. From those ports, the iron started its journey by sea to all parts of Britain and the rest of the world. Some ships carried rails for expanding railways in the UK; others took iron for the same purpose as far away as Russia for building the Siberian railway. The iron was also in great demand for armaments and ship building. Merthyr Tydfil, with its iron works that had started at the end of the previous century, was at the heart of the industrial revolution in Wales.

But by the middle of the nineteenth century, a great shock hit the iron manufacturing industry. In 1856 Henry Bessemer patented a process for producing malleable iron, using a blowing cylinder, without recourse to coal or charcoal. The Bessemer process, as it became known, was the dawn of the steel age and although no one then could forecast the impact the development would have, it was the beginning of the end for the mass-produced iron manufacturing age.

The glory of the great Merthyr ironworks district was fading; a slow burial by technical and economic changes in manufacturing processes, but the iron industry was not yet finished for those willing to take their chance in the North of England.

Klondike!

Around the late 1840s and early 1850s, men in the iron works of Merthyr Tydfil were hearing stories of big developments going on in the North East of England from iron workers who had already left Wales. The development of the railways and shipbuilding in the North East generated demand for good quality, readily available iron. That demand was behind the emergence of the great works in Consett and later Middlesbrough.

The expanding railway system was also the means by which people came to work in the North East from all parts of the UK. Tales trickled down to Merthyr Tydfil of two men who had become business partners and opened an iron works on a greenfield site, Witton Park, near Bishop Auckland. One of these men was John Vaughan, a former Dowlais iron worker, born in Worcester of Welsh parents. The other was Henry Bolckow, a German businessman who had become a naturalised British subject.

In what seems now to be a complicated series of moves, Bolckow and Vaughan initially brought ironstone from Whitby into Middlesbrough and transported it west to Witton Park. They had begun to build the Witton Park Ironworks in 1845. The site had been chosen because of its close proximity to a source of good coking coal and plentiful water. The development of the railways in the North East had made a reasonable business proposition out of the movement of iron and people to such places.

Within a year of opening up the site, Witton Park No.1 Blast Furnace was put into action, smelting ironstone there before it was transported back to Middlesbrough as pig iron, a type of cast iron.

Pig iron had its name from the layout of the series of moulds coming from the main stream of molten iron. Some imaginative soul thought this layout resembled a pig (the main stream) suckling its piglets (the individual ingots forming along the length of the stream). Brittle pig iron was further processed in forges, foundries and rolling mills to eliminate the impurities from it so that it became stronger and, therefore, more suitable for making everyday metal goods and parts for bigger projects.

Teesside iron was used to expand the railways throughout the area, to build locomotives and to build and replace bridges, such as the iron bridge in Sunderland. Iron from Teesside was used for the water supply pipes in London. William G Armstrong, later Lord Armstrong, the founder of the College of Physical Science that was to become Newcastle University, invented and manufactured the first lightweight breech-loading iron and steel gun as a response to the difficulties that soldiers had experienced in manoeuvring heavy field guns in the Crimean War.

In 1850, there was a great discovery. Iron was found in the Eston Hills near Middlesbrough. This was a significant economic find as it was nearer and easier to access than the iron from Whitby.

Many of the iron men in Merthyr Tydfil left for the North East and what they hoped would be better work and prospects in County Durham and North Yorkshire. Handpicked men were taken there by their managers. Francis was amongst them. At one time in the 1800s it was reckoned that two fifths of the skilled iron workers in County Durham and Teesside were Welsh. They were joined by other hopeful characters from Scotland, Ireland, East Anglia and Staffordshire.

Francis Lewis gravitated towards the iron works at Witton Park in South West Durham. This small place to the west of Bishop Auckland was a focal point for the throng of Welshmen travelling up to the North East from Merthyr Tydfil in the mid to late 1850s. The ironmasters in the North East were paying top wages of £2 to £3 per week and providing decent housing right next to the works.

The iron rush had begun.

Work and life in Witton Park

I knew nothing of Witton Park or its significance in my ancestry, even though I had grown up only a few miles away in the same county. From the 1840s onward, a village called Witton Park was purpose-built to serve the developing ironworks. The blast furnaces formed an incongruous monument to industry in an otherwise rural environment. By 1867, there were seventy-six puddling furnaces and two mills courtesy of Bolckow & Co Ltd. Working these furnaces, men in Witton Park made possible major engineering projects worldwide.

The man in charge of a puddling or reverberatory furnace at an ironworks was known as a puddler. It doesn't sound much to puddle, or stir vigorously, the molten pig iron in the furnace, but it was skilled work, learnt on the job. Through puddling, the brittle pig iron that was created in a blast furnace was converted into the more useful wrought iron. Puddling was conducted at high temperature (1300°C). The vigorous stirring was done with a heavy rabbling-bar, a long iron rod with a hook at one end. The impurities in the molten pig iron oxidised to form various oxides or slag. The slag rose to the top of the furnace. At the same time, oxides of carbon and sulphur were given off as gases. As the impurities were removed from the iron, the melting point of the iron increased and the metal became a spongy mass of wrought iron. The puddler knew from the feel of the metal on the end of the rabbling bar the right moment when the pig iron had become wrought iron. This wrought iron was then rolled into equally weighted balls by means of the hook on the end of the rabbling-bar. The metal balls were wheeled out white hot to the 'shingling hammer' with which any remaining slag was beaten out and internal fissures fused together.

The flattened iron that resulted from the puddling was fed into grooved rollers in the rolling mill and shaped into cylindrical rods or flat bars. These rods and bars were then rolled out, sliced into lengths and re-stacked, and the whole process repeated many times until wrought iron of the right quality was finally produced.

All of this manoeuvring of the iron had to be performed in the face of searing heat and the white-hot slag which spurted out with each slam of the massive hammer. Furnace men were skilled and strong men who had to have good concentration. They would not have been clad in safety gear in those times. In their woollen trousers and vests, they risked each day being badly burnt by molten metal. Working in unnaturally high temperatures, they were easily identifiable by their 'sunburnt' look and the white scars from the sparks that flew at their inadequately-covered arms and faces. A man could lose several pounds in weight through dehydration by the end of a shift. Breathing in the foul, gas-laden fumes and then cooling down rapidly at the end of a hot sweaty shift took its toll on those who worked in front of these fiery furnaces. For many, it dramatically shortened their lives.

Perusal of the Witton Park census returns for 1861 and 1871 reveals a community made up of strangers drawn from all parts of Britain and Ireland with a few from further afield including France. There were Welshmen in over half of the houses in some of the streets in Witton Park. Many of those men had brought Welsh wives with them, others had married English women on their journey north or once they had reached County Durham. In some families, the birthplaces of the children formed a reminder of the route their fathers and mothers had taken on their way to Witton Park.

This little Welsh community far away from Wales carried with it its language and customs. Welshmen lodged alongside other Welsh families and Welsh would have been spoken in many homes and between men at work. But, although they may have started out as Welshmen, they were gradually converted into Durhamites, albeit with a strong sense of their Welsh roots.

The Welsh chapel-goers, Presbyterians, Congregationalists, Baptists, and Wesleyans, built places of worship in the North East in the 19th century. Witton Park had its share of those chapels. With the chapels, came the Welsh-speaking preachers and the eisteddfodau, annual Welsh artistic competitions especially involving singing and poetry.

The hopefully-named Zoar Baptist church opened in 1857. Zoar, a neighbouring place to Sodom and Gomorrah, was spared being consumed by fire and brimstone on the day of judgement. Ironically, the sulphur fumes and smoke from the constantly burning furnaces, the dust and dirt from slag and nearby coal mines, the soot from household chimneys together with the constant noise of hammering, might have made an unfamiliar observer think that they were already in a kind of hell. To those who lived and worked there, the sights and smells were normal, as were the associated lung complaints from inhaling the fumes and the burns from the furnaces and molten slag tipping.

With the Welsh, too, came choirs, more formally in chapel and informally in the public house. Witton Park was known for being the only place for miles where you could hear a bit of good singing. As typifies Wales and the Welsh, there was the ever present tension between the culture of the public house and that of the church or chapel. On the corner at the bottom of High Thompson Street there was a public house called The Welsh Harp, a place where, no doubt, many wage packets would have been converted to drink long before they reached home. Elsewhere in Old Row there was Iron Works Inn next door to a Welsh Wesleyan chapel, temptation and redemption within a couple of steps.

By 1860, Francis had met and married a woman ten years his junior, Isabella Bird from Thornley, County Durham. Francis and Isabella were married in one of the oldest surviving and best-kept Anglo-Saxon churches in England, the parish Church of St John the Evangelist in Escomb. Witton Park was in the parish of Escomb.

Reproduced from an original postcard, printed by Judges of Hastings, www. judges.co.uk.

At first, Francis and Isabella lived in Thompson Street, Witton. The street was thronged with men and their families who all depended on the iron works for their existence. In Thompson Street alone, there were forty men working as puddlers. There were furnace heaters, boilersmiths, blacksmiths, engine drivers, shinglers, ballers, slag tippers, mill furnace men, and labourers. Living alongside in the same street were tradesmen and women serving some of the needs of the iron men and their families: a butcher, a tailor and draper from Dorset, dressmakers, washer women, two cordwainers (makers of fine shoes), a grocer and draper, and a boot and shoemaker.

As many did before and after this time, Francis and Isabella first lived with his wife's parents, William and Margaret Bird, and four of Isabella's younger siblings. The Birds had lived in Witton Park for over ten years after moving from Kelloe, near Thornley, County Durham, when Isabella was a little girl. Perhaps Francis had met Isabella by lodging with or nearby her family. The Birds and Lewises lived closely in three rooms in the last but one house in Low Thompson Street, a Yorkshire-born boot and shoe maker on one side and a grocer and draper from Redcar at the end house.

William Bird, born in Jarrow, was a blacksmith in the ironworks where Francis worked. Looking at Francis' marriage certificate and then the birth certificates of his children gave me an insight into his employment. Francis was an iron heater at the time of his marriage. The following year he was a baller. A heater attended to the furnaces used for heating metals for forging, rolling, hardening and tempering. He would maintain the furnace at the correct temperature and withdraw the heated metal when it was ready for its designated purpose. The baller worked alongside the furnace man (puddler) and came into action when the metal began to solidify; at this point the baller divided the metal into separate malleable balls. Once this had been done, the balls were handed over to the shingler, who directed a large and heavy hammer worked by steam or water power. By repeated blows, the shingler brought the rough hot metal to a more compact form for the rolling mill. These jobs were skilled work and better paid than Francis' mining job in Merthyr Tydfil. By 1862, Francis had become a furnace man.

On 2 April 1871, Francis and Isabella were living in 27 Albion Street, Witton Park, an even more Welsh enclave than Thompson Street. Living in this long street were scores of Welshmen and their families. Surnames such as Thomas, Lloyd and Owen abounded. Even if the census return had not given the places of birth, you would have known that over three quarters of the households were Welsh; names like Owen Bowen (derived from Owen ap Owen meaning Owen son of Owen) and Thomas Powell (Thomas son of Howell) were typical. Many men had come from the industrialised parts of Monmouthshire and Glamorganshire such as Nantyglo (brook of coal) and Dowlais. There were others, fewer in number, from North, Mid and West Wales. Thomas Richards and Richard Thomas lived near one another, no doubt causing confusion to some less Welsh neighbours!

Albion Street, full of iron workers, was a little further away from the iron works than Thompson Street. Apart from a butcher and a woman who did washing, there was not much by way of services here.

Francis and Isabella by now had four children: Mary, Rachel, William Francis and Margaret. The Lewis family plus Francis' sister-in-law and a boarder, John Griffiths from Merthyr Tydfil and his French wife, all lived together. Nine of them crammed into the three-roomed house. However crowded this might appear, it may have seemed relatively sparsely populated compared to some of the lodging houses nearby. As many as 40 lodgers were reported in one house in Bishop Auckland, with men, women and children all sleeping together. In places such as this, the beds never had chance to cool down before another worker came off shift and jumped in for his rest.

The Lewis' neighbours in Albion Street were, on one side, a 30 year old widow from Staffordshire, her family of four young children and two boarders. The young widow's tale was a common one. She would have come to this place with her husband. He would have come because of the work, an iron roller, full of optimism. Within a few years life had changed out of all recognition. There she was, miles from home with no husband, her source of income gone, alone with four small children. All she could do was to take in boarders to help pay their way. On the other side lived a Welsh couple, their niece and two boarders. Francis, like many in this street, was working as an iron heater once again.

Francis and Isabella's first child (Mary in 1862) and fourth child (Margaret in 1871) were born in Witton Park. In between, in 1864, Rachel was born in West Hartlepool and in 1869 William Francis was born in Darlington. The older children did not have much schooling. Mary could not write. She made her mark rather than signing her name when registering her son Charles' birth in 1881 in South Bank. However, as we shall see in future chapters, the only son, William Francis, was quite literate.

I wondered why the Lewises had moved about before returning to Witton Park in 1871. I suppose it is possible that Francis stayed in Witton Park and that Rachel and William Francis were born elsewhere because Isabella went to stay with relatives when she was expecting those two children. That hypothesis is supported by the fact that she was the parent who registered both Rachel and William Francis. However, she also registered Margaret in Witton Park so I do not think I can sustain the hypothesis. In 1876, Francis registered the birth of the last child he and Isabella were to have: Alice Esther born in Middlestone Moor just south of Spennymoor in County Durham. At the time of Alice's birth, Francis was no longer working in the iron industry but was a collier labourer. In carrying out wider research about the economic state of the iron industry around 1860 to 1880, I found that the times when the family appeared to be living away from Witton Park coincided with strikes or down-turns in the iron industry. As the factory owners reduced wages when trade turned down, the workers might go on strike.

The most obvious reason for the moving around would be for Francis to seek work. His employment track record and changes of address seem to show a man who would work wherever and at whatever was needed to put food on the table. But reading something of what was happening in Witton Park in the 1860s and early 70s made me wonder if there could be another reason.

As we saw in Merthyr Tydfil, the iron industry was susceptible to boom and recession years. The strong men who had been taken on in Witton Park would stand up for what they believed to be their entitlements for their hard labour. If they felt that they were being short-changed, then they would not stand for it. There were many rebellions and strikes when the iron masters wanted to reduce wages at times of recession.

At the height of the iron works production in the 1850s to the early 1880s, there were some 4,000 people living in Witton Park. On the fortnightly pay days, it would regularly become a place of heavy drinking as men rushed to spend their hard-won cash in one or more of the many public houses. There were three public houses in Thompson Street alone. Wives would have tried to track down their men to extract money to buy food for the next two weeks before it was all converted into beer. Local factions and disagreements would come to the fore and the two policemen paid for by the iron masters would have been totally inadequate to deal with the disorder that could ensue. There were frequent disagreements and fights between the Welsh and the Irish. Also, the Irish would fight fellow countrymen who took opposing views regarding the cause of independence. The magistrates in Bishop Auckland had no fear that they would ever become redundant.

Despite long since being an illegal practice, the iron works issued some of the men's earnings in the form of truck tokens (locally known as 'tommy tickets'). These tokens could be exchanged for goods from the shop owned by the ironmasters. In families where the men had a problem with drink, this was the only way some women and children had any chance of getting food. The experience of truck tokens William Francis would have known about as a boy would come back to him later in life when confronted with something similar in another place.

On 2 November 1866, to add to the usual level of excitement, there was a riot in Witton Park. The factory owners had taken on new workers at the iron furnaces to cover for men who had been on strike since the July of that year. The men had been on strike after the ironmasters had imposed a 10% pay cut.

When men went on strike in Witton Park, they not only gave up their employment, but they could be driven out of their homes too as the houses belonged to the iron masters. So, unsurprisingly, the men on strike took the blackleg action very badly and showed their outrage in, '...*various acts of a most disgraceful character*'. For taking part in the riot, two men were tried at Durham assizes and sentenced to six months imprisonment. The strike ended in December. The men had won nothing and lost a lot. They went back to work with the pay cut that the masters had demanded in the first place. They were able to have their homes back and in a magnanimous gesture agreed that the blacklegs could have the empty homes in the village.

Which side of this situation did Francis find himself? Had he left Witton Park because of the recession and sought his fortune further afield? Had he been one of the two men sent to prison? Knowing what my father would have done in similar circumstances, I am inclined to think that Francis would simply have upped and offed in search of something elsewhere rather than going on strike. This, I think, is the reason we find the family at the addresses in West Hartlepool and Darlington. Both these places had iron works in which Francis would have found work. Francis' occupation is given as a mill furnace man at the birth of Rachel in West Hartlepool and as a furnace man at the time of William Francis' birth in Darlington. Their addresses in West Hartlepool, 3 Hope Street, and in Darlington, Havelock Street, were both deep in iron works territory.

A change of fortune

Finding Francis on the 1881 census return took me nearly as long as finding him in 1851 when he had left Abergwili. For years I had been side-tracked by help from a fellow ancestry hunter from a family history society to which I belonged. My helper had persuaded me that Francis had left his wife and was living as someone else's husband in Park Terrace in Stockton on Tees.

My family history society co-member told me that he had looked up Francis on the 1881 census return of April that year. He told me that Francis from South Wales and his wife Mary from Copley, County Durham were living at 7 Park Terrace Stockton with the head of the household - a 34 year old commercial traveller called Henry Binning, Henry's blind sister, Elizabeth, and their servant. Rather puzzlingly, Francis was described as the father (of whom it was not clear although I assumed it must be the head of the household) and his occupation was coal merchant. I was told by my co-ancestry hunter that he could explain the puzzle as he had also found a marriage in 1866 of Francis and Mary (nee Binning). The fact that the children were named after their mother and not their father suggested that Mary had had the children to a former husband.

In the absence of any alternative, and with some encouragement from my co-researcher, I felt that this must be 'our' Francis. For years, I wove an increasingly bizarre story around these 'facts'. Francis must have left his first wife whom I knew for certain to be Isabella Bird. As Isabella was still alive in 1881, I knew Francis could not have been a widower free to marry Mary Binning so either he must have divorced his first wife (unlikely for someone of his station at that time) or he had lived bigamously with his second wife. I also thought Francis must have changed his line of work as he had been an iron worker at the time of his marriage to Isabella and when my grandfather was born. Perhaps this was to cover up the fact that he was living a lie? I occasionally thought that there must be another Francis Lewis born in South Wales in 1828/29 who had been in or around Stockton at the time of the 1881 census, but however hard I looked it was a fruitless search. Adding further to the riddle was the fact that I could not find my 11/12 year old grandfather on the 1881 census. The joint mystery lay there for years with my harbouring thoughts of a bigamous rotter of a great grandfather who had walked out on his wife and children. Quite what he done with my grandfather, heaven only knew!

Jumping forward some 20 years, and using my recently purchased subscription to an internet search site, I decided to look again for Francis Lewis on the 1881 census to see if earlier transcripts had missed out anyone of this name. Much as I had not really felt that the one we had found was the right one, I still did not find anyone other than our coal merchant. However, I noticed the search facility on the site had an option for seeking variants. Clicking on the variant options for first and surnames, I then found something very interesting. With the variant surname box ticked, up came a Francis Lewig, mill furnas (sic) man aged 51 and son Wm F Lewig scholar aged 11. The two of them were boarding with an iron miner and his family in New Brotton, east of Middlesbrough. This Francis was from Wales and Wm F was born in Darlington. The enumerator's handwriting was not the best but even though I looked for other names he had written ending in an 's' there was no getting away from the fact that it was Lewig and not Lewis. Nevertheless, despite the incorrect surname, I felt sure that these were my forebears and the mystery of the bigamous coal merchant and his missing son was solved. Francis Lewig is described as being born in N Wales, Carmarthenshire. However, when you look at other entries made by this enumerator what appears to be a capital N is more likely to be a capital W, as something similar appears at the start of surnames like Nilliams, Nood, Nells and Nellington!

My mystery was solved and my apologies were made mentally to my great grandfather. But finding that Francis, Isabella and their children were no longer living together led me to speculate as to why this should be.

Francis, it appeared, had moved once more with the work, this time taking his only son with him. Francis was back in the iron works, as a mill furnace man once again. Although William Francis is described as a scholar on the 1881 census, it is quite likely that at the age of 11 he was working alongside his father as had happened in Merthyr Tydfil with fathers and sons.

Perhaps Francis' work was not secure and he could not support Isabella living with him in Brotton. Maybe there were other reasons for them being apart, personal or financial. Whatever the reason, Isabella was living at 5 Branch Street, South Bank, Middlesbrough with her youngest daughter, 5 year old Alice Esther. Isabella was working as a charwoman and had taken in two lodgers who would have provided some additional money. These men both worked in the iron industry. One was a Welshman from Swansea and the other a Durhamite from Winlaton near Gateshead, home of one of the oldest forges in England.

Mary, known as Polly, the eldest of Isabella and Francis' children was married at 17 years of age in 1879. In 1881, she was living with her older blacksmith husband Robert Foster and their first child, also Robert. They lived in Napier Street, Normanby in Middlesbrough, not far from her mother.

Isabella and Francis' second daughter, Rachel, aged 16, was working as a general domestic servant. Rachel was living at 41 West Street, Normanby with her maternal grandparents (William and Margaret Bird), one of her aunts (Mary D – her mother's sister), her aunt's husband (Joseph Craig) and their baby (Thomas).

Margaret Lewis, the third of Isabella and Francis's children, aged 10, was staying with an aunt (Sarah Bird) - another of her mother's sisters, in Willington, Co Durham. Probably, Margaret was an unpaid servant to her aunt.

It was quite clear that as soon as the children were old enough to do some form of work, they were farmed out to where they could be most useful. Schooling did not seem to be high on the agenda.

Breathing in dust and working in extremes of temperatures were everyday hazards for those who worked with iron and coal. Even living in those industrial areas was hazardous enough. The air was filthy with smoke, dust particles and noxious gases. Breathing problems and lung diseases were common. Late in 1881, the 30 or more years that Francis had spent in the iron works took their toll when he became seriously ill with bronchitis. Being ill and unable to work, he would not have been able to support himself or his family. His only option would have been to accept poor relief. The nearest thing to a hospital for those with no money was the dreaded workhouse. Francis was admitted to the nearest workhouse in Stockton on Tees where he died on 7 December 1881. His remains were buried in the churchyard of Stockton Holy Trinity Church.

I was very touched by finding out about Francis' sad end. I felt he was a man who had strived hard all his life in some pretty unspeakable surroundings and yet, at the end, he had died in the workhouse away from his family from something that nowadays would have responded in a few days to a course of antibiotics.

With my only experience of a workhouse being courtesy of Oliver Twist by Charles Dickens and various filmed versions of that book, I wanted to know more about how things would have been in a workhouse about that time.

Attitudes to the poor had changed over the years. If we look back at Francis' grandfather, John, we see one attitude: that those with more money and status in society should do their bit to help those less fortunate than themselves. By 1834, a new Poor Law had brought with it a view that the poor were poor largely as a result of their own actions and that if they so desired they could change. The way in which poor relief was administered was a key thing that changed as a result of the new law. It dealt with the temporary or longer-term relief for people who had fallen on hard times for a variety of reasons, such as old age, illness or having no means of supporting oneself. However, high on the new agenda was the deterrence of idleness. Unmarried pregnant women who were disowned by their family could only go into the workhouse to live before and after the birth of their children. The mentally ill or mentally handicapped would often be placed in the workhouse, away from the rest of society.

Entering the workhouse must have been a humiliating experience. The new entrant would have to strip and be washed and then clothed in the workhouse uniform. The clothes the person came in with would be given back when, or, more likely, if, the person left the workhouse.

Workhouses generally had a small infirmary room or a block for the care of sick inmates. Poor Law unions were responsible for the administration of the Poor Law in an area that usually comprised a number of parishes. The union had to employ one or more suitably qualified medical officers to tend to the union's sick, both inside and outside the workhouse. The post of medical officer was not always a particularly attractive one. Until 1842, posts could be put out to competitive tender, with the appointment generally being made to whoever demanded the lowest salary. This meant that applicants were often the least experienced members of the profession or those with private patients who would invariably take priority over the poor. Apart from attending patients, medical officers would also have to pay for any medicines they prescribed. Unless the officer was particularly altruistic, it cannot have been in his interest to prescribe much, especially as there would be few people looking out for the patient on a personal basis.

Early nursing care in the union workhouse was usually provided by female inmates. Women would find it in their interest to seek out this work as they would be rewarded with a better diet than the other occupants and also be given beer to drink. When the nursing staff carried out duties such as laying out the dead or especially repulsive tasks they were also given a glass of gin which the medical officer was expected to sanction. Some workhouse masters were in the habit of distributing intoxicants to these inmates early in the morning. Alcohol was a commodity that could be traded in exchange for money or other goods to those with a taste for it. Unsurprisingly, many of the nursing inmates were intoxicated throughout the day. Coupled with the fact that few of them could read, mistakes were commonly made when dealing with labels on medicine bottles. Before 1863, not a single trained nurse existed in any workhouse infirmary outside London.

In the 1860s, pressure began for improvements in workhouse medical care. Amongst the most notable campaigners were: Louisa Twining, a prominent figure in the Workhouse Visiting Society who devoted many years to helping the poor who were sick; Joseph Rogers, a medical officer who wrote in his Reminiscences of a Workhouse Medical Officer, a courageous, graphic and critical appraisal of conditions in the Strand workhouse in London; and the rather more well-known Florence Nightingale. The medical journal, The Lancet, also played its part.

In 1865, The Lancet began a serious of detailed reports about conditions in London's workhouse infirmaries. Its description of St George the Martyr in Southwark was typical of what it uncovered and there is no evidence to suggest that things were any better in Stockton:

'Each ward had an open fireplace; a lavatory and water-closet in a recess or lobby; in some instances the latter served for two or three wards. In several cases the grossest possible carelessness and neglect were discovered in some of these wards. Take the following in illustration:—Thirty men had used one closet, in which there had been no water for more than a week, and which was in close proximity to their ward; ...In No. 4 ward (female), with 17 beds, the drain-smell from a lavatory in a recess of the room was so offensive that we suspected a sewer-communication, and soon discovered that there was no trap; indeed it had been lost for some considerable time. Apart from this source of contamination of the ward, there were several cases with offensive discharges: one particularly, a case of cancer, which, no disinfectant being used, rendered the room almost unbearable to the other inmates. ... The absence of the usual decencies and needful cleanliness of the infirmary will at once suggest the class of nurses in charge: for we feel assured that no properly trained nurse would have tolerated such abominations as we witnessed. The number of the sick and infirm amounts to between 200 and 300, all of whom are nursed by pauper nurses, who receive in money from 1s. to 2s. per week, meat and beer daily, and dry tea and sugar.'

In 1851, Stockton Union Workhouse was in Portrack Lane. The main building was originally a U-shaped layout and contained male accommodation at the east and female at the west. Children were housed in a separate block at the south of the site and an infirmary block stood at the south-west. Vagrants' wards lay to each side of the entrance.

The buildings were later expanded. A central wing containing a dining-hall was added at the rear of the entrance block. A further ward block was erected to the south, and a large new building for male patients was erected in 1868 at the south-east of the site. Another block, probably for isolation cases, was built to the south of the original infirmary. Later in the 20th century the workhouse became a hospital before closing in 1970.

So, having braved the journey from his native rural Wales, survived the awful conditions in iron mines and furnaces, given life to a new generation, Francis died alone in a place of shame and dread.

Bereavement and a broken home

As awkward as it can be searching for the right people in census returns and other records, this is relatively straightforward compared with trying to ascribe reasons for the actions of those no longer with us, or trying to work out what relationships might have been like within the family and wider community.

What did I know? My father, Kenneth, knew nothing of his Lewis grandparents. Why would this be? Was my father's father, William Francis, ashamed of them, or did he dislike or fear them so never spoke of them? Well, almost certainly Francis' family would have been ashamed to know that their father ended his life in the workhouse as this was something feared by all working men and women who had no means of support but their own labour. The fear of the workhouse, even in a semi-jokey way was passed down through the next two generations. As late as the 1960s, my father would say, in jest, but with enough of a hint of concern, that we would have him in the workhouse if we asked for anything expensive.

I have no reason to think that either Francis or Isabella were feared or disliked by their children. The Christian names, Francis and Isabel(la) were given to their children's children, something I do not think they would have done if they had feared or disliked their parents. In the case of my grandfather, he gave the name Francis as one of the names of his first born son and Isabel to his first surviving daughter.

My view is that the family simply had to work to survive and if that meant the family splitting up to seek work elsewhere then that was how it was. Children had to grow up early in those days.

Whatever the situation was after his father had died, William Francis Lewis, by then aged 12 had to go home to live with his mother and youngest sister, Alice Esther. Shortly after Francis died, Isabella moved from Middlesbrough back into County Durham, nearer to her parents. There, in April 1882, she married a widower, Caleb Burgess, who was nine years her senior. Another iron worker, Caleb was originally from Dudley in Worcestershire. Caleb's wife, Mary, had died in 1877 aged 43 when they were living in Tudhoe, County Durham. Caleb had been left on his own with five children: Richard, Frederick, Caleb (junior), Ellen and Emma. No doubt, the marriage was of mutual convenience.

Caleb and Isabella moved back to Teesside after they had married. By 1891, only Caleb junior of the true Burgesses was living with this father and stepmother at 46 Holden Street, Grangetown, Middlesbrough. Isabella's mother Margaret had died. Also living with Caleb and Isabella was William Bird (Isabella's father), Alice Esther, wrongly described now as a Burgess, and Isabella Foster, the 4 year old granddaughter of Isabella. William Francis was no longer with the family. At the age of 22, there was no reason to think he would be, but I also think that he may not have got on with his stepfather, perhaps for the reasons given in the next paragraph.

My father's cousin, Isabel Fox (daughter of Rachel Lewis) told me in the 1980s when she was an old lady that she remembered Caleb senior as a cruel character. Rachel's and William Francis' mother, Isabella, died aged 55 in 1895. As with Francis, the years of filthy air had taken their toll and she died from bronchitis and also cardiac dropsy. Caleb lived to be very much older, eventually dying aged 85 from what would probably be described nowadays as dementia. He died in the then mental asylum in Sedgefield. His medical records have survived and are an insight into the kind of detail that was recorded about patients deemed to be mentally ill in the early part of the 20th century.

Every aspect of Caleb's cranium, ears, hair and heart was noted along with intimate details of his alimentary, respiratory, vascular, genital, and nervous systems. He was 5 foot 1 inch tall and weighed 6 stone 10 pounds.

The hospital records describe his mental state as: '...*very noisy – swearing and continually talking about damnation.*'

The copy of the medical certificate describes him as '....*extremely violent, struggled and yelled incoherently at the top of his voice, kicked the cell door and was unable to realise in the least his general surroundings. John Wilkinson (special constable) 36 Wellington Street Stockton on Tees states that he was extremely violent when brought to the police station, he kicked him (Wilkinson) on the leg and shouted and yelled at the top of his voice. Michael Flynn, Police Sergeant, Stockton on Tees states that he has been dangerous for some time running after children and throwing stones at them also spitting at people without provocation.'*

Despite his reputation, I read this record with some degree of sadness wondering how dangerous an 85 year old man just over 5 feet tall and weighing less than 7 stone can have been.

A soldier's life

At the time of the 1891 census, there is only one William or William Francis Lewis born in Darlington in 1869 who is recorded as living in the whole of England or Wales. That William was working as a steam engine fitter and lodging along with others with one Hannah Lewis (Welsh and from Carmarthenshire but no proven relation) in Lock Street, Darlington.

After much thinking and hypothesising, I have come to the conclusion that it is unlikely that this person is my grandfather. The reason for my thinking this is that some years ago I visited Kew Record Office and found his army record papers. On 14 May 1889, just after his 20th birthday, my William (Francis) Lewis had enlisted in the regular army at the regimental depot in Richmond, North Yorkshire. He signed up for twelve years (seven with the colours and five with the reserve) with the Royal Horse Artillery. He was a gunner trained to fight on foot and to ride and look after horses in the heat of battle.

His army record shows he had already served with the 4th Battalion the Yorkshire Regiment. I found out from the Green Howards Museum in Richmond that this regiment was part of a network of ancient militia or reserve forces made up of volunteers.

William Francis Lewis was living in Oliver Street, South Bank, and working as a labourer in one of the local factories when he joined the 4th Battalion. He would have trained one or two nights a week in the local drill hall under the command of a former regular soldier. The volunteers were known as 'Saturday night soldiers'. In the early 1800s, these men were a bit like a local voluntary police force but later, around 1875 to the 1890s, the battalion concentrated more on drilling and hardening up young men through training and bonding. Each year, an annual training camp was held in different parts of the North Riding, an enjoyable adventure for young men who had probably never ventured further than the local streets in which they lived. Through the camps and training, many of these territorials had been used to firing guns and following orders since they were 15 years old. Some progressed into the territorial force having been with organisations like the Church Lads' Brigade. They were not paid a wage but did receive a small payment known as a bounty. They had two types of uniform – khaki for work and red for best. Not all would have the uniforms as they had to pay for them themselves. The men would turn out and march for local celebrations and church parades. The best of the men from the militia were recruited for the regular army.

William Lewis' army medical pronounced him to be: fit, height 5 feet 9¼ inches, weight 138 pounds, chest measurement 34 inches, fresh complexion, light grey eyes, light brown hair, and of the Church of England. Although he was 20 years old at the time of enlisting, his age is said to be physically equivalent to a man of 19 years and 4 months. Clearly according to some army formula, he was rather slight and underweight for a 20 year old.

His army number, 73473, was fascinating to him as the numbers were either 7 or could be made to add up to 7. He regarded 7 as his lucky number.

William is described as having served all of his seven years 'at home'. Part of his time he was based in Ireland at the Curragh in County Kildare. At that time, Ireland was still counted as home service. I assume that the reason I have never found him on the 1891 census was because he was in Ireland at the time.

At some time in his service in Ireland, he had a photograph taken in Dublin, shown on the following page. He is wearing his dark blue Royal Horse Artillery uniform.

When I was a child, I was given two jigsaws that must have been in the family for quite a while as they seemed second hand even then. These jigsaws emerged every time we had miserable wet days that were not fit for playing outside. They were both part of a set called, The Toby 250 piece Military Series of Jig-saw Puzzles. They each depicted a single soldier in full dress uniform standing in the foreground against a distant background of his colleagues rushing into battle. One was of a soldier in a green uniform and the other, which I still have, shows a soldier in the 10th Hussars in 1808. Despite the time that the jigsaw depicted,

I imagined the soldier in the picture to be my grandfather, especially when I saw the picture below.

Photograph of William (Francis) Lewis in 1890s in the dark blue braided uniform of a gunner in the Royal Horse Artillery

During his service with the colours, he was a gunner and for a short time was promoted to the rank of bombardier. He completed seven exemplary years with the colours on 14 May 1896. By then, his mother had died (November 1895) and he was discharged to live with his aunt (Esther Thomas née Lewis) at the White Ox Inn in Abergwili, South Wales.

Becoming Welsh

William's life in Wales started with a name change. Perhaps there were rather too many William Lewises around. But whatever the reason he henceforth became known as Francis or, more commonly, Frank.

Having left the army, he needed a job. He changed his army uniform for that of a water bailiff, a policeman of the waterways and river fishing rights. He patrolled the River Towy, often at night, looking for poachers of salmon and sewin (the Welsh name for sea trout) much prized by the locals. Frank had to be fit to catch these men, many of whom would have been ready for a fight. Armed with stocks and clubs to kill their contraband fish, they were not averse to lashing out at anyone trying to part them from their source of income. But Frank's job as water bailiff was a fill-in until something better came up.

It did.

On 25 July 1897, just over a year after arriving in Wales, Frank Lewis was aged 27½, height 5'10". Now with a proportionate figure, an understanding of Welsh, particular marks of large flags on the front of his chest and cross flags and a crown on his right forearm, Frank joined the Carmarthenshire Constabulary as a 3rd class constable. His police number was 7.

Life was fairly quiet and he was able to spend time with his cousin Miss Mary Valentine Thomas (pictured here, second from left at front) for whom he had developed a soft spot.

Mary was some eight years his junior, the only daughter of Mrs Esther Thomas of the White Ox. Living under the same roof, Frank and Mary were able to get to know one another very well, but under the gimlet, hooded eye of his aunt, Mary's mother.

Within a year, on 25 July 1898, he had progressed to being a 2nd class constable based in Llanelli and all was going well. His work as a policeman was very much the usual run of dealing with drunkards, petty thieves, fighting, domestic abuse and poachers, with some of whom he had no doubt made acquaintance in his role as water bailiff.

The local press (Llanelly and County Guardian) reported cases brought by named police officers as a special weekly feature.

Month after month, PC W F Lewis brought case after case of drunks to court.

17 March 1898: *'James Evans Mount Pleasant Bldgs and Wm Davies Zion Row, both of Llanelly were charged with being drunk and disorderly in Upper Williams Street on the 2nd inst. PC W F Lewis said that he saw the defendant in Upper William Street about 11.40 pm. Both were very drunk and wanted to fight with two other men. The defendants were fined 15s each including costs.'*

Cases involved as many women as men, as was recorded on 28 April 1898 under the heading of: A Chatty Defendant. *'PC W F Lewis charged Mrs Dymoch Gwyn Terrace Llanelly with being disorderly and refusing to quit the Cornish Arms on the 20th instant. The constable was called to the Cornish Arms about 6.15 pm on the day in question to eject the defendant. He asked her to go out before the constable came, and added "You please tell the truth." She then went on to tell the Magistrate a long story to try to explain how the whole affair had happened, but she was cut short by the Chairman who told her to come to the point. She finally stated that she had borrowed a shawl from Mrs John, the Cornish Arms. One day when it was raining, she wore the shawl again and went into the Union Inn to have a drink with some other lady friends. Whilst here, Mrs John sent over to her to say she wanted to see her. She went over shortly afterwards to the Cornish Arms and Mrs John asked her to give her shawl back. Witness refused, and said she wanted it to go home because it was raining. Both parties then had some sharp words, and Mrs John told the witness to go out of her house.*

The Chairman asked if Mrs John was in court. The constable said she was not. The Chairman thought he would like to hear what Mrs John had to say, and instructed that she be sent for.

On arriving, Mrs John went into the box and said the defendant had borrowed her shawl and when she came to her house she asked for it back, but she had refused to give it, so she told her to leave the house. She then got very abusive, and called her names.

Defendant: Oh you liar. Turning to the bench she said "She is a falsehood, and telling what is false."

The defendant then became very excited, and talked nineteen to the dozen until the Chairman stood up and shouted "5s and costs."'

The following month on 26 May 1898: *'At the Police Station on Friday morning before Messrs Samuel Bevan and Thomas Jones, PS John Harries charged Ann Llewellyn, Llanelly with being drunk in Union Terrace, Llanelly on the previous night. The officer said that shortly before midnight he saw the defendant in Union Terrace, unaccompanied by another woman in a terrible state of intoxication. They both went back into the back premises of the Royal Park Hotel. Witness went after them and asked them what they were doing there, and defendant replied that they were not doing any harm. He ordered them to leave and the defendant subsequently went in the direction of Spring Gardens where he lost sight of her.*

PC W F Lewis said that at 3.15am that morning he found the defendant sleeping in a truck on the Bres Crossing. He awoke her and she said that she felt giddy and had laid down. Thinking that the police station was the best place for "giddy" people he locked her up, and on searching her found a bottle containing liquor about her. She was fined 5s and costs, in default 7 days. She asked to be allowed time to pay and was given a week.'

The type of cases brought and the way in which they were tested is a telling tale of the times. Reading them made me wonder when the police had decided to find it acceptable for people to be drunk on our streets and ignore them.

A case such as one on 17 November 1898, when William Francis was based at Llanelli police station, was more serious: *'Aggravated assault on a wife. At the Police Station on Monday morning, before Mr Thomas Jones, John Williams 5 Railway Place, Llanelly (sic), was brought up by PC Wm Francis Lewis, charged with cutting and wounding his wife on Saturday night.*

PC Lewis stated that about 1.45 a.m. on the 13th he saw prisoner's wife at home with her head bandaged up. He examined her, and found a cut, apparently fresh, just above the left temple, which looked a nasty one. It appeared to have previously bled. In consequence of the complaint she made, he went downstairs and arrested prisoner and charged him with cutting and wounding his wife that morning. When handcuffed, the prisoner stated, "I have done nothing, my wife knocked her head against it." [Stay with it reader to find out what 'it' actually was]

Ann Williams the complainant (who appeared very weak and had to be provided with a seat) said that between 11 and 12 on Saturday night last, the prisoner was in bed with her. He accused her of having improper relations with a man who had called to buy mussels. She then got out of bed and went downstairs. The prisoner afterwards threw the contents of a bedroom utensil over their eldest son William. She went upstairs and asked him what he had done that for, and he struck her with the utensil on the left side of the head. She lost consciousness and would have fallen had not her daughter Harriet caught her. She thought he had killed her, she bled very much. She was sure he hit her intentionally as there was a light in the room.

Cross-examined by the prisoner, Complainant stated that she did not strike him while he was in bed. It was not true that she struck her head herself.

Prisoner was then remanded until Wednesday.

Bail being applied for, the complainant objected to allowing the same, as she was in bodily fear of her husband.

Upon condition that the prisoner would not go near his wife, bail was allowed in two sureties of £10 each.

The case was resumed on Wednesday, when Dr Alfred E Brook, assistant to Dr D J Williams, said he saw Mrs Williams about 3.30 on Sunday morning. He examined her and found a contused wound over the left frontal region, some laceration of the skull, and the hair around matted with blood. It was possible that such a wound was caused by a blow with such a utensil.

In answer to the Chairman, the witness said the woman was suffering from a certain amount of shock, but he did not think the wound was one to do grievous bodily harm.

Mr Russell Howell, dispenser with Dr D J Williams, said he saw the complainant about 12 o'clock. There was blood on the bed on which she was sitting, and also on her dress. There was a swelling on the left side of her head above her ear, and a slight cut about an inch long.

At this stage the Chairman said the Bench were of the opinion that the defendant did not commit the deed with intent to commit grievous bodily harm, and therefore it would be discharged, and the charge reduced to one of aggravated assault. The defendant not wishing to have an adjournment the case was proceeded with.

Harriet Williams, daughter of the complainant and defendant, was called, and said that shortly after she got to bed she heard her mother scream, and going into her mother's room, she saw blood flowing from her mother's head. Her father was in the room, and he was in the act of putting the utensil down when she went into the room.

John Williams, a son of the defendant, also gave evidence, and said that both parties were quite sober when the assault was committed.

The defendant, in defence, said that on this particular night he went to bed and complained that the children ought to be in the house earlier, when his wife immediately got out of bed, lighted the candle and began beating him. The defendant in self-defence caught hold, of the utensil and the complainant ran against it in her excitement.

This concluded the evidence, and the Bench retired to consider their verdict. After a few minutes absence they returned, and the Chairman said that the Bench had given very careful consideration to the case, and they had decided to fine him 40s and costs, or in default 14 days In coming to that conclusion, they had tempered justice with a great deal of mercy.'

I did not know whether to laugh or cry when I read the above. The coyness in referring so euphemistically to the 'utensil' which had caused such harm to the defendant is laughable. Also, the ease with which an unlikely explanation tempered the sentence reminded me of a woodwork teacher I once had to interview after a child had complained to me that he had thrown a saw at her in class. He told me that she was not paying attention and he had inclined the saw in her direction and she had not got out of the way sufficiently quickly before it glanced at her!

Looking at the census for 1901, I was pleased to see that Ann appeared no longer to be with the wielder of the 'utensil'. Although still described as married, she was now the head of the family of her four remaining children.

On 27 April 1899, William Francis brought yet another of his drunks before the magistrate after being attacked as he made the arrest: *'William Williams, Treboeth near Morriston, a middle aged man, was charged with being drunk and disorderly in Station Road on the previous Saturday night.*

PC W F Lewis stated that he saw the defendant in Station Road shortly after eight o'clock in a very drunken condition. He was causing a disturbance and had a large crowd around him. The constable ordered him to "move on", but defendant was not in a mood for being ordered about and became very abusive with the result that the witness had to take him into custody. Defendant on the way to the police station struck the constable with his stick and kicked him several times.'

Williams had to leave 23s 6d with the Magistrate for his 'night out'.

Life ticked over in this vein, but within a few months life was about to change in a very big way for Frank, so much so that he might well have preferred to have a couple of kicks and hits with a stick from a drunk one Saturday night.

War!

In early October 1899, PC William Francis Lewis was called up to serve in the army as a reservist in a war. He might have expected to live peaceably (well, as peaceably as a policeman could) through his five years as a reservst. In the event, he managed nearly 3½ years before being called upon. As he changed his police uniform for an army uniform, he could reckon on at least 18 months' service if the war continued for that long.

The war in question was the South African War, sometimes known as the 2nd Boer War, or the Anglo-Boer War.

Frank left for South Africa on 24 October 1899, once again a gunner in the Royal Horse Artillery. He left his cousin Mary a gift of a tiny, two-part set of a Book of Common Prayer and Hymns Ancient and Modern. The burgundy leather books were four inches by two inches in size and were contained in a similar leather case. Inside of each he had written, *'There's gladness in remembrance'.*

He would have been hoping that this war would last as short a time as the first Boer War (just over three months) but the signs even then were not good.

He would have known something of the troubles in South Africa. For weeks in the local

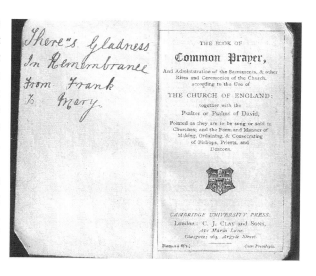

press, alongside the articles about the cases he and his fellow policemen brought to court, there were many items of news about local people who had gone out to live in South Africa. Having emigrated to better themselves, many found that they were increasingly caught up in unrest and certain war.

To understand why Britain was at war in Africa, I had to find out something of what had gone on in South Africa in the preceding forty to fifty years. Until undertaking this research, my only knowledge, if that is the right word, of historical warfare in Africa was gained by repeated Christmas viewings of Zulu!

To find some answers, I looked as far as I could at the accounts of the war from different sides. I looked at contemporary accounts and those viewed with hindsight from the second half of the 20th century. My mission was to find out why the British army found itself at war in Africa at the end of the 19th century. It will be of little surprise that the reasons can probably be boiled down to politics, money and men's ambition. What follows is a very much potted version, a scene setter, of what scholars have written volumes on over the years.

For centuries, the whole of Africa had been fought over by European peoples including the British, the Dutch, the Portuguese, the Germans and the French. But for the purposes of this part of the story, I go back to the late 1830s and early 1840s to a time when about 15,000 people of Dutch extraction moved out (the Great Trek) of the Cape Colony established by the British across the Gariep (Orange) River into the interior of South Africa. They did so, according to observers at the time, because they rejected the British philanthropic view of the rights of the native African people which proposed the equalisation of black and white at the Cape. They also disliked the political marginalisation they experienced on the eastern Cape frontier.

The Voortrekkers, as these migrants were known, settled and established themselves in the Transvaal and the Orange Free State. The Voortrekker republicans were subsistence farmers, rather like their African neighbours, within their newly annexed territories. The settlers became known as Boers, an Afrikaans and Dutch word for farmers.

The British Government recognised the independence of the two states at the Sand River Convention for Transvaal (1852) and the

Bloemfontein (1854) Convention for Orange Free State. Transvaal became the South African Republic with a single stipulation from the British: that there should be no slavery. The Orange Free State had been territory Britain had occupied for eight years. When the British withdrew, it was an unpopular move. So much so that the British Government voted £48,000 compensation to those who might have suffered from the change.

Within a decade, huge deposits of diamonds had been discovered around Kimberley in the Cape Colony and on the borders of the South African Republic. The subsequent diamond rush, with fortune seekers pouring in from other parts of South Africa and elsewhere, ended the Boers' isolation.

During the 1870s, the British annexed that part of the territory where the Kimberley diamonds lay. Five years later, the British tried to extend their influence by appropriating the Orange Free State and the South African Republic into a federation of British and Boer territories. The Boers resisted this. When the South African Republic declared independence from Britain, the 1st Boer War started.

The 1st Boer War was probably caused by three underlying factors: a desire by Britain to control trade routes to India via the Cape; discovery of huge mineral deposits within the South African Republic in the Cape Colony near the border; and Britain's continuing race against other European colonisers with similar interests.

That war, which began in December 1880, lasted just over three months. The British tried to annexe the South African Republic (Transvaal). The British were the losers. They were met by a type of opposition that they had not experienced before.

The Boers did not have a uniform but instead wore dark grey, neutral or khaki farming clothes. Each man brought his own single shot breech loading rifle. These men were skilled marksmen, snipers, used to making a single shot count from a great distance when hunting game. The Boers blended into the terrain that they knew so well and proved to be excellent opponents to the British infantry who were like sitting targets in the African landscape in their uniform of red jackets, black trousers with red piping down the sides and white pith helmets. In the last battle of the First Boer War, the British had a 46% casualty rate; the Boers lost one man and had six wounded, one fatally.

This outcome, and how it had come about, had a great effect on the British army for subsequent wars. Never again would British soldiers fight in red uniforms, changing instead to khaki so as to blend in with the background. Highland regiments in Natal devised aprons to conceal coloured kilts and sporrans. Regiments learned the danger of anything that would make their soldiers stand out, such as shiny buttons and too-flashy signs of rank which had led to disproportionately-high officer casualties.

Lessons would be learned, too, about the Boer marksmanship, their tactics and use of ground.

At the end of this war, Britain agreed to Boer self-government in Transvaal under a theoretical British oversight. The Boers accepted the Queen's nominal rule and British control over African affairs and native districts.

But, in the mid-1880s, the world's largest gold-bearing ore was discovered on the Witwatersrand in the Transvaal. A conservative estimate at the time put the value of the gold at £700,000,000. Many thousands of prospectors poured in from all over the world to seek their fortunes. Very many of them were from Britain. Amongst them were managers, engineers, miners, traders and business people. Initially the money to run the mines came mainly from England, but as time went on German and French interests became similar to those of the English. The numbers of uitlanders, as these incomers were known, were such as to outnumber the Boer community.

Several attempts were made by the uitlanders, both peaceably and aggressively to acquire the rights they felt they had earned. They were not only denied a voice in relation to the mines they had opened, they had no voting rights, no control over education, no power of municipal government, they were debarred from jury service and they were heavily taxed into the bargain. Yet, the uitlanders provided about $7/8$ of the revenue of the country. Some liberal Boers were in favour of granting citizenship and justice to the uitlanders. However, they were outnumbered by hardliners who felt that the uitlanders should not only wait on probation for this honour for 14 years but also give up nationality of their former countries thereby rendering the incomers stateless. By

April 1899, the uitlanders appealed to Queen Victoria to either protect them or acknowledge that their protection was beyond Britain.

The scene was inexorably set for a bloody exchange both at a government and a personal level. No doubt, too, the lure of gold made it worthwhile committing the vast resources of the British Army and the huge costs in what became the 2nd Boer War.

The Boers, under Paul Kruger, struck first. They went into the Cape Colony and Natal between October 1899 and January 1900, successfully besieging the British garrisons in the towns of Ladysmith, Mafeking (defended by troops headed by Robert Baden-Powell) and Kimberley. They inflicted three separate defeats on the British during 10 to 15 December 1899. It was not until reinforcements arrived on 14 February 1900 that British troops commanded by Lord Roberts could launch counter-offences to relieve the garrisons. The relief of Mafeking on 18 May 1900 provoked riotous celebrations in England. The British moved on to the Orange Free State and took Bloemfontein on 13 March and then onto the South African Republic (Transvaal) where they took the Boer capital, Pretoria, on 5 June.

Although the bulk of the heavy fighting was over by then, Boer units fought as guerrillas for nearly two more years. The British, now under the command of Lord Kitchener, responded by constructing blockhouses, destroying farms and confiscating food to prevent them from falling into Boer hands. The British placed Boer civilians in concentration camps.

The use of concentration camps has cast a long shadow over the history of the British in South Africa. The camps had been originally set up to act as places of refuge for people made homeless by the war. However, when Kitchener took over from Roberts in November 1900, the war tactics changed as he sought to get rid of anything or anybody who might give sustenance to the guerrillas. Using a scorched earth policy, Boer farms and their crops were destroyed, wells poisoned, livestock slaughtered and fields salted to prevent any regeneration of life. A whole nation was targeted. Whole regions were depopulated. As farms were destroyed, the Africans who had lived with the Boers were made homeless too and they were interned in separate camps from the Boers.

About 28,000 Boer men were captured and many were sent abroad. The remaining people in the camps were mainly women and children;

26,000 of them died in the camps. At one point, there were over 90,000 Boers in the camps and nearly 25,000 black Africans. The conditions in the camps were unacceptable from the start. Insufficient food, poor hygiene and inadequate sanitation all led quickly to diseases of want and of infection.

Political opinion back in Britain was very much split with those who thought that the camps were an outcome of war and those who were uneasy about the reports that were reaching them about the scale of the camps and conditions in them. An all-woman commission was set up to investigate the state of affairs. The commission's report led to an improvement in the conditions in the camps until the death rates were lower than in some British cities, but by then the damage had been done.

The war finally ended in May 1902 when the last of the Boers surrendered. The Treaty of Vereeniging signed on 31 May 1902 ended the South African Republic and the Orange Free State as independent Boer republics, placing them instead in the British Empire. By 1910, the Union of South Africa had been established as part of the Commonwealth.

What, I wondered, had been Frank's role in all of this?

Motion sickness and a great discovery

This is the point where I have to explain the link between my having motion sickness and my great family history find regarding Frank Lewis.

One Saturday morning in Llanelli library, I was looking for Lewises on census returns on a microfilm reader. I can only look at these films rotating around the screen for about thirty minutes at a time before motion sickness sets in and I have to stop. My half hour was well and truly up when I had a walk around the library to distract myself from how I was feeling.

I wandered over into the corner of the library where I found someone's life's work in a polished-wood card-index cupboard. Here, some dedicated librarian had indexed all of the stories in the Llanelly and County Guardian going way back into the 1800s, each entry hand written on a slip of paper and neatly filed. I found myself searching for anything on William Francis Lewis in the index. To my surprise, I found something that was to lead me to an even greater find.

I came across two articles in the index: one headed 'Homecoming at Ammanford' dated June 1901 and another 'Honouring a Comrade – police rally round PC Frank Lewis', dated 22 August 1901. I could scarcely believe what I was reading. Forgetting my motion sickness and the abandoned microfilm reader, I ordered the huge bound volumes of yellowing newspapers and turned to the pages in which these articles had lain undiscovered for over 80 years.

I found descriptions of the hero's welcome that Frank received on returning from the Boer War. I then started to look back through the newspapers to find out more about the Boer War and to my even greater surprise, I found a series of letters that Frank had sent to people at home from the seat of war in South Africa. Those people had passed on the letters to the newspaper for publication.

I can do no better than to share with you details from these letters as a first-hand account of the war.

The start of Frank's war

The first letter from Frank was sent to his sergeant in the police force in Ammanford and his sergeant's wife. The letter was written on 30 November 1899 from 1st Cavalry Brigade, Ammunition Column, Naaupoort in the Cape Colony, South Africa.

In this letter, Frank gives his first impressions of South Africa and offers a few lessons in Afrikaans' pronunciation. He also gives an immediate feel for the concern he has about his fate.

'Dear Sergt and Mrs Davies

I write you these few lines hoping you and the family are in good health, as it leaves me at present. We arrived in Cape Town on the 18th and disembarked on the 19th, and proceeded at once up to this place, called Naauport (pronounced Nowport). We were 48 hours in the train, coming a distance of 619 miles. The horses, of course, had to be watered and fed frequently on the road, and the road is also very hilly. In places it is a narrow gauge railway. The country was very nice at first when we passed through, being a wine producing country, but for the last 400 miles it is exactly like a desert, sandy with short bushes all over and what they call the Veldt (pronounced felt), with kopjes every few hundred yards (small, hills varying in size). We are 69 miles from the Free State Border. It is a junction here with a few houses and a couple of stores on the main line from Port Elizabeth and one line branches off to Colesburg and thence into the Orange Free State and on to Johannesburg way, while the other line goes on to a junction called De Aar and thence to Kimberley. The Free State Boers have invaded Cape Colony. They were down here before we came, but have not been since.

When we came here we had to cross a big bridge a little way from here, and just after we crossed it someone blew it up. We had only just cleared it, so we had a good start, had we not?

The Boers are entrenched just outside Colesburg, and are about 5,000 strong. We have had a couple of skirmishes last week, but only slight affairs. We had four wounded. We are waiting for more troops as we are not strong enough yet to advance. Lord Methuen has been giving them beans at Belmont with his brigade of Guards.

I wonder how Joe-ty-Glasson has fared. We get very little news here. I have no idea when we will return. If I am spared I expect we will be making a general advance next week, so by the time you receive this, goodness only knows where we may be. Dead perhaps! You never know your luck. I think I have told you all the news this time, give my regards to all my comrades, I will now conclude with kind love to you all.'

Frank and his regiment, the Royal Horse Artillery, had left Britain via Aldershot and Southampton in late October 1899. The men and their horses spent many days at sea. Once in South Africa, they travelled over 600 miles in a train for two more days to reach their first posting.

Frank's belongings were packed into a wooden trunk about three feet by two feet and eighteen inches deep, W F Lewis and RHA painted on the side in white letters. I still have this trunk. For years it had lain gathering dust and grime in Dad's sister's coal house. By the time my cousin and I retrieved it, the base was rotten but the rest had survived the last century intact. It has now been restored and is a repository for family history papers and photographs.

With General French

Frank's war efforts were reported again a month later on 25 January 1900 when another letter to Sergeant Davies and his wife appeared in the Llanelly and County Guardian.

This one is headed by the newspaper, 'With General French - Where are all the Llanelly crack shots?'

'Dear Sergeant and Mrs Davies,

I write you these few lines hoping yourselves and family are enjoying good health as I am at present. I hope you all spent a happy Christmas. We did not have much chance here, but still we made ourselves as happy as possible under the circumstances. No doubt many of us will not see another Christmas day.

You will, of course, know about the heavy fighting we have had at Colenso and other places, and of our severe losses, but we must take the good and bad; we cannot expect to pursue a war without getting some reverses, and there is no doubt we will have our own back again. I thought myself it would be all over before our lot got out here, but we have been landed over five weeks, and the enemy are still in Cape Colony. So far I think we have had the heaviest fighting in the campaign on this side and we still have some heavy fighting before us.

I am now with General French's Brigade, and we are camped at Arundel, 10 miles from Naaupoort. I have put the address Naaupoort. If you should write it will be forwarded to me. We came out here on the 7th December, we had to drive the Boers out, and captured a good herd of sheep and cattle. We have had some heavy fighting or skirmishes. The Boers always fall back, and try and get us on to where they are entrenched. We caught a few of them one day behind a Kopje. Next morning we were sent there to reconnoitre, and we found six wounded and forty dead. We buried them there and brought the wounded into camp. The Boers are about 5000 strong at Colesburg, whereas we are only 2000, but now we have been reinforced to about 4000 strong so we will be soon having a good smack at them. We have had some hard work, sometimes with very little to show for it, and still losing one here and there.

I had one very narrow shave, a bullet striking the saddle in front of my thigh.

There have been some wonderful close shaves. One fellow had the top of his water bottle shot off, and another the butt of his revolver shot away; and one of the New Zealanders was killed – shot dead by a Boer 1000 yards away – you can see they can shoot a bit straight.

Where are the Llanelly crack shots? Send them out here. There are a great number of sad homes this Christmas in England, Wales, Scotland, and Ireland after some loving one who had fought for his Queen and country, and is now buried in the veldt in South Africa. From Orange River to Kimberley is the scene of many hard fought battles and skirmishes and the graves of many brave officers and men, and there is no doubt there will be many more before Kimberley and Ladysmith will be relieved.

Although we have had one or two reverses, we will show them yet what we can do. We are true British soldiers and we are determined to fight to the last, until we will conquer the Boers once and for ever.

I received the Llanelly Guardian with the sad account of the sudden death of Capt. Scott, a thorough gentleman. Believe me, I failed to read the account, a comrade had to do it for me. It completely overcame me for the moment although I am a soldier, in a country where dead and wounded are to be seen daily. If I shall be spared to return to Ammanford, I shall find that Mr Picton Phillipps will have been removed to Llanelly, and that will be another sad loss. But I hope that Mr Johnny Phillipps will be appointed superintendent; I believe he will make a very good one, like his brother.

Please write, and let me have all the news. Try and send me the Llanelly Guardian every week, if possible. I shall feel very thankful to you. Give my regards to all enquirers, and accept the same for yourself and children.

Yours faithfully,

Franck Lewis (No. 73473)'

When I first read this letter, I thought that the Scott to whom Frank refers was Captain Scott of the Antarctic, but I realised that this could not have been so. He could have been referring to one of two men of that name who had died in the defence of Kimberley, one the commandant of police who, in his humiliation and grief at being unable to defend his post, had shot himself. The other was Scott-Turner who was killed by the Boers in the siege of Kimberley. In the absence of anything more likely, I might have settled on either of these two Scotts as being the one whose death had upset Frank so much. But one day whilst looking for some other information, I found a reference to a Captain

Dalkeith Martin Scott, a military man originally from Kent but living in Llanelli with his Australian wife. This Captain Scott was a well-regarded man with more than his fair share of civic responsibility. From his mid-thirties, Captain Scott was both the Superintendent of police and the Chief Fire Officer for Llanelli. Perhaps those dual responsibilities took their toll as he died suddenly aged 45 in late 1899. His death was widely reported in the newspapers that friends back home sent out to Frank. It seems much more likely that this was the Captain Scott to whom Frank refers especially as the Mr Picton Phillipps, mentioned by Frank, took over from this Captain Scott.

I wonder if Frank later cringed at knowing his letters had appeared in the newspaper, especially with his thoughts on the promotion prospects of one of his police superiors there for all to see. One can only hope that Mr Johnny Phillipps did indeed gain his promotion otherwise Frank might have had some explaining to do to the alternative incumbent.

Perhaps I do the editor a disservice, but I did speculate if the request for the Llanelly Guardian to be sent out each week had been inserted as a bit of self-advertising on the behalf of the newspaper.

Dodging the bullets

As if Frank's views on police promotions in the previous letter were not enough, the following week on 1 February 1900, the Llanelly and County Guardian published another letter from our man which was rather damning of the army. The letter had actually been written before Christmas on 18 December 1899 to a policeman friend, PC Jones in Llandeilo. PC Jones allowed the newspaper to print the letter sent from camp in Arundel. Its content was clearly not vetted in any way.

'...I am still in the land of the living; have managed to dodge the bullets up to date. No doubt, all England is ringing with our severe losses and reverses, but I hope it won't continue long; it is the stupidity of our officers in charge. There are many hundreds of poor fellows gone under in the last two battles Methuen has fought; someone is continually blundering. Gatacre has made a mess of it, and we are now having news of Buller's defeat and the loss of eleven guns. That brigade left Aldershot two days before us; they were in the same square as we were in. They have lost very heavily, and it is sad to hear of the loss of our guns, but I hope we will have a bit of luck, and change the course of affairs a bit.

We have been at it night and day for nearly a fortnight; rather hard work under a hot sun, and sleeping on our arms all night; and we have not much to show for it yet. The beggars scoot as soon as we get in range. We have had a few casualties, of course, but not many. We have had a few of the enemy; we killed over forty one day in quick time. The first shell R Battery, RHA, fired in the campaign struck a Boer fair in the chest, and tore him to pieces almost. How was that for finding the range? But they, too, are very fine marksmen, I can tell you. One of the New Zealanders was sent out to cut some barbed wire the Boers had put up, and he was shot dead by the Boer at 1,000 yards, but they had marked the range before. Another had the butt of his water-bottle shot away. I don't know whether you saw it in the papers, but at one engagement one of the fellows lifted his helmet up a bit over a rock, and he had a bullet put through the centre of it; and another put out his hand to grasp his rifle, which he had laid down, and his hand must have been visible, for he had two bullets put through *his hand immediately. So you see they have not forgotten to shoot straight, but we will have our own back before long, I hope. We are holding our own in our division, which is more than some can say, and we have about 6,000 opposing us – three to our one. We have had to retire once or twice pretty quick, but we have always managed to drive them back. Last Wednesday they tried to flank us, and get to our base and stores at Naaupoort, but we gave them beans before they had gone far.*

We expect to start every day on Colesburg, where they are heavily entrenched, and then to Bloemfontein. No one can say they are not fighting pluckily, for they fought desperately at Magersfontein. I don't know when Methuen is going to get to Kimberley, but he has lost a lot of men. We have a hard nut to crack yet in Spyfontein. Baden-Powell has done splendidly in Mafeking. Has he not kept them at bay splendidly? But everyone, I think, is doing his best to uphold the honour of our country, and , although we are having the worst of it so far, only let us get a fair smack at them, we will give them what for, I'll bet.

I have been away for two months. I never thought I should be out here three months ago, but one never knows his luck. Perhaps it may be my luck next to stop a bullet. There are hundreds who have got a lonely grave out here. The Gordons and the Black Watch have suffered fearfully at Magersfontein, and above half of them reserve men. An awfully unlucky lot are the Gordons; the other battalion suffered heavily at Elandslaagte. We buried a few last week; two officers on Sunday – one of the Caribineers and one of the 10th Hussars. They were both shot dead. No doubt we will lose heavily before we get to Pretoria. Christmas and New Year's Day will have passed before you receive this.'

The Gatacre referred to was the commanding general of the British forces at the Battle of Stromberg in which 135 men were killed and 696 captured during a single ambush.

Buller was General Sir Redvers Buller, a dynastic general of the old school used to riding out with thousands of men which proved to be disastrous in the early fight against the Boers at Ladysmith and then at Spion Kop. He became known as 'Reverse Buller' amongst the troops and was eventually replaced by Lord Roberts.

Only on re-reading this letter for the umpteenth time did it dawn on me that the fighting may have been taking place in our winter but, of course, it was high summer in South Africa.

Graphic and pathetic narrative

Another letter from Frank to a friend in Abergwili, written on 7 January 1900 from Rensburg, was reprinted in the local paper on 15 February under the heading of 'Graphic and pathetic narrative'. It is interesting to see the change in meaning of the word pathetic with how we might use it today.

'…We are at a place called Rensburg. It is only a siding on the Cape Government Railway. There are only two or three farms near at hand, and this place is named after the owner of one. His name is Van Rensburg, and he has joined the Boers. He has also raised about 300 recruits for them. His brother, also a Van, was going to join them but he was caught by one of our patrols. So much for Rensburg.

We left Naaupoort (pronounced Nowport) on December 7th for a place a few miles below this called Arundel. We had a pretty good battle before we drove them from around this place. It was on some kopjes: here we found 40 dead Boers, whom we had been firing at the previous day. We then pitched our camp here, and have been fighting heavily every day since Monday. A good start for the New Year, was it not? We were 24 hours without water at the beginning, and had only two biscuits to eat during 36 hours. We were fighting continuously, and the Boers must have lost heavily, for we have driven them back bit by bit.

During Monday and Monday night it was a very anxious time, but about 6pm on Monday it was seen that we had won the Battle of Colesberg. However, we have not been able to occupy Colesberg yet, and if we had the enemy we would have cut the lines of communication. We first want to drive them away and get them in front of us. They keep to these kopjes, and the country is full of them, and very picturesque they look.

The Life Guards are here. They came in yesterday. They are out today, and have had a baptism of fire, having lost four men and an officer – a captain. We had one bad disaster yesterday. Two companies of the Suffolk Regiment were detained to prevent the Boers getting supplies, as we had them partially surrounded on Friday night, when we provoked fighting but during the night the Boers surrounded them, and yesterday morning when dawn broke the Boers opened fire on them. The colonel and four officers were killed, and six others either wounded or prisoners, and 167 men killed and the rest wounded. They were 280 strong going into action, and only one officer and six men have returned as yet. The colonel had the top of his head blown off, and the adjutant, no one could recognise him. His face was literally full of holes where the bullets had struck him. I helped bury 30 men and the six officers. We dug a trench to bury them in, and lay them fifteen aside. We put the Colonel on two [probably should be top], and two officers each side of them.

We obtained the body of the Colonel from the enemy under a flag of truce, and many of the Boers came down and assisted us to bury then, and sang hymns in Dutch over the graves. It reminded me of dear old Wales. They said they were sorry to see the Dutch and British at war with one another, and pitied us, but the big people in London were to blame. They also said there would be many such graves as this one before we entered the Free State territory. A major was reading the burial service, but broke down completely before he had finished. It was an impressive and sad scene there amidst the lonely veldt and kopjes, and the sun's rays covering them as they lay in their last resting place, such as I never want to see again, and my thoughts wandered back to dear old peaceful Abergwili amidst the hills and valleys of beautiful little Wales, which the scenery put me in mind of, and I could not help but feel sad for those away in Britain, who would be watching and waiting for their loved ones whom they will see no more, for the Suffolks came out 1,100 strong, and had over 600 reserve men, and the majority had their time in during this month, and nearly all married. Ah, well! Such is war. Only those who see the field after a battle can realise what it is, and to see the number of Boers lying dead too is sickening at times.'

It is well documented that the troops were poorly looked after on their journey through the Cape Colony to the border with the Orange Free State and onwards to Pretoria in the Transvaal. The troops marched on little food and water. Where there was water, it was not plentiful and the quality of it was occasionally vile, taken from places where bodies of horses and men had fallen. With no protection against the tropical sun during the day, or against the almost arctic cold at night, they were understandably tired and not always in the best of shape. Given all this, they were determined to go on and overcome their enemy.

By the beginning of April, Frank and his brigade were in Bloemfontein in the Orange Free State having a short rest before pressing on some 250 miles to Pretoria.

'…*during the past few months we have been at it continually, first around Colesberg way, where we had some hard fighting during the month of January, and did some good work there under General French. Of course, all I can tell you, you will have read long before now in the papers. We were at Rensburg on the 3rd of February, when we went with General French to Modder River, where there was a large army marching under Lord Roberts and Kitchener. We were there until the 11th of February, when we set off with our Brigade under French for the Relief of Kimberley. We marched off at 2.30 a.m. on the Sunday 11th, and crossed the Free State Border at 11.30 a.m the same day, and on the 15th inst. we relieved Kimberley, getting in at 8.40 p.m. We had some hard fighting and marches, and suffered greatly from the heat and thirst. On the 18th inst. we took part in the Battle of Paardeberg, which lasted from dawn on the Sunday and raged fiercely all day until darkness came on and subsequent days until the 27th, when Cronje surrendered.*

Our losses were very heavy for the Sunday, especially in the Highland Brigade, who had over 300 killed, wounded, and missing. I saw 93 of the Highlanders buried Monday and Tuesday in one grave, and the other Regiments lost heavily too. The Welsh was one, and the Cornwall's. The heat was terrible all day, we suffered very much with thirst, being many hours without water. After Cronje's surrender, we rested until the 6th of March, and then set out for this place – Bloemfontein – and after some hard long marches and three hard fights, we captured and entered the Orange Free State, after only firing two shells on the 13th of March.

Our Brigade were first in, as it was at Kimberley, the clocks marking 1.20 p.m. as we passed the town to our Camp, about a mile beyond, where we have been camped ever since, with the exception of a week when we were about 15 miles further up, at a place called Glen Drift, where the Boers had blown up a fine bridge crossing the River Modder. We had on a big engagement about ten miles from there, called Brandfort, but we soon played havoc with them, and next day we left there for our old Camp here, I believe the Batteries that took our place had a disaster near there, one Battery losing five guns and all the men, with the exception of seven.

I hope this War will soon be over now, for it is just six months since we had our papers, and I have not slept in a tent since we left the Modder River on the 11th of February, only the stars for our covering, and at times our hardships have been great, many days having one biscuit each to last all day. We had to go 25 miles and fight nearly all the way, and be as long as 22 and 36 hours without water, and then be glad to drink water out of the river full of dead horses and bodies. We had to tighten our belts two holes for dinner and then the same for tea. One or two biscuits a day don't tend to make a man fat do they, but we bear it as well as we can for it is for Queen and Country and our duty, and we try and do it as well as we can, even though we find a lonely grave under the shadow of some kopje.'

The dates included in Frank's letter deserve closer examination to appreciate just what he went through in those six or seven weeks.

Between the beginning of February and the middle of March, Frank and his brigade would have travelled at least 300 miles, some of it on foot and some by rail. A typical day's march was 20 miles with fighting alongside on some days. Often, they walked 25 or even 40 miles a day when already exhausted, underfed and lacking water. Although part of the Royal Horse Artillery, Frank would have been like an infantryman who could ride a horse rather than a cavalryman.

Before the Relief of Kimberley, a force of some 3,000 men was taken by rail to Belmont, south of Kimberley and then by road to Ramdam, twenty miles north east of Belmont. Here they joined others making a larger force of about 5,000. In the early hours of 12 February, they set off towards the Modder River which lay between them and Kimberley.

This being summer in South Africa, the heat was great and the soldiers were only sheltered by the dust bank in which they road. They rode all day on 13 February over the dry veldt until men and horses drooped with the heat and the exertion. Men and horses were parched. Horses and mules which pulled the guns fell and died from exhaustion. By the time they reached Kimberley, they had come 100 miles in four days with insufficient food and water. It was not uncommon to see men falling out or troopers walking and carrying some of the saddle gear to give their horses some ease.

Kimberley was relieved on 15 February 1900 by General French making a spectacular gallop across the Veldt with his cavalry division. In this dramatic action, a high proportion of the cavalry horses, overloaded and unused to the conditions, were lost leaving the cavalry division seriously weakened. French lost 500 horses in one day during the relief of Kimberley. The life expectancy of a horse once it had landed in Port Elizabeth was six weeks. A memorial exists in Port Elizabeth to the 300,000 horses that were killed during this war. It shows a horse being given refreshment by a soldier kneeling before the tired looking beast. Its inscription states: *'The greatness of a nation consists not so much in the number of its people or the extent of its territory as in the extent and justice of its compassion.'*

The unprecedented number of horses which died was due to several factors. The horses were not acclimatised or rested properly on arrival in South Africa; they were made to carry too much; and many of those in charge of them were inexperienced in their management.

There was no time for the troops to rest on their laurels after Kimberley. It was onwards to Paardeberg, east along the Modder River to cut off Cronje's connection with Bloemfontein in the Orange River State. There were already some 25,000 foot soldiers and 8,000 horse soldiers with 98 guns mustering on 12 February. Seven hundreds wagons drawn by 11,000 mules and oxen came up behind. All of this army with its associated animal power were gathered in a fairly foodless and waterless area.

Frank was one of fewer than 2,000 men who accompanied General French out of Kimberly at 3.00am on the following Friday morning. There had originally been 5,000 men but so many horses were unfit to carry anyone that the force was drastically reduced. It is said that horses actually died under their riders, but still the force marched on for 30 miles. The fight in which they found themselves was hard. As the day wore on, there were 1,100 reported killed.

The Battle of Paardeberg lasted until 27 February when General Cronje surrendered. Contemporary accounts of the battle are striking. The loss of fifty British men is described as, *'another small disaster'* (Sir Arthur Conan Doyle). But the other thing that comes across is the devotion to Lord Roberts ('Bobs' to his men) and the officers' and men's determination to beat *'old Cronje'*.

Typhoid!

We do not see any more published letters from Frank in the paper until September 1900 when we see a letter written a month before on 14 August from near Middleburg in the Transvaal. It is clear from this last published letter that Frank has had a hard time of it in what is now winter in South Africa.

'…I have been very ill with fever, but I am all right again, thank God, though it pulled me down terribly, as I had it very severely, and received only indifferent treatment whilst sick; in fact, no attendance whatever, and was lying on the floors of empty houses and sheds, with only one blanket the whole of the time. You will no doubt have seen the account of the Hospital scandal, so you will have an idea what the treatment is like, and what we get when whilst sick. I can only add that it is only too true what Mr Burdett Coutts M.P. writes, but I hope it will be rectified soon.

We have lost thousands of lives out here from disease, far more than the number killed by enemy's bullets, and I say it is very sad indeed. So you see when we have not had the enemy's shells and bullets to face, we have had a more dread enemy to face in 'disease'; but I hope I may be spared to return home safely again – but we can never tell what a day may bring forth. We see the sun rise in the morning, but we cannot tell whether we shall see it set or not.

This campaign has, and is, lasting longer than anyone thought it would, and yet we cannot see any signs of the end. It may collapse in a week, and it may last some time yet. Our hardships have been great and trying, especially the last few months, for it is winter out here, and the nights are so fearfully cold that it generally freezes hard, and such cold piercing winds! It is very trying to bivouac with only the heavens for a roof in all weathers, and only one blanket to cover us, and a waterproof sheet under us, and we had no winter clothing until about a month ago, when we got some winter khaki which has been much appreciated, I can tell you. I hope the war will not last much longer. I know we are all anxious to see the end of it, but I expect we will have some severe fighting yet up this way, as the enemy are concentrating a few miles up above us under Botha, and we expect to have another smack at them sometime this week.

People at home cannot realize the hardships a soldier has to endure as we have had to do in this remarkable campaign – ill clad and ill fed, and bivouacking under all weathers and under short rations, as we have done; but still we have tried to do our duty, and have shown the whole world that we are still what Englishmen were in the days of yore.

I joined this battery on the 7th of April at Bloemfontein, and we left there on the 1st of May, marching from 6.30 a.m. until after midnight to join this brigade which is commanded by General Hutton, a most capable and kind leader, who considers his men always. This brigade is all mounted infantry, and composed chiefly of Colonials. We have had Canadians, New Zealanders, Tasmanians, and Australians, and other Colonials, as well as our own mounted infantry. We fought in five actions, and were specially commended by Bobs for turning the enemy right at Vet River, and on two other occasions where we turned the enemy's flank when they had intended to make a stand against the main body.

We have had some very hot and heavy engagements indeed, notably at Zand River and by Johannesburg, at a place called Oliphant's Vlei. We have two days' awful fighting there on the 28th and 29th of May; it was there I had to go sick. I had been ill and could go no further, but I really thought we should be all wiped out there during the whole two days, the fire was something terrific. I was sorry I had to go sick as I would have liked to have gone to Pretoria with the troops, but I joined them there later on, and we have had some terrific fighting with Botha since Pretoria was taken, both at Diamond Hill and from a place called Oliphant's Fontein up to Middleburg, which we occupied 28th July.

We had another hot fight at a place called Whitpoort, when about 1,500 Boers attacked us just at daybreak; we were only about 300 or 400 strong, and we fought them all day until dark, and had at one time a 35 mile firing line against us; that is to say, from one flank to the other flank of the Boers it was just 35 miles, but we drove them off just before darkness set in. But we had a belly full that day all round and our casualties were pretty numerous, and the Boers must have lost heavily also. I am glad and happy to state to you that the story about me being wounded is false, I have been indeed fortunate to come through so many hot engagements without being hit, and I hope I will do so to the end.

We have been slogging at it now ever since we first struck off with general French around Naauwpoort and Coleberg way, and from there to Modder River and then to Kimberley, Paardeberg, where we saw the surrender of Cronje and his force, and then to Bloemfontein, and from there to Kroonstad, and on to Johannesburg and Pretoria, and now up here we are about 90 or 100 miles from Pretoria, on the Delagoa Bay line. The Boers are some 30 miles away at a place called Belfast. I suppose we will pull up at Lydenburg, where I hope it will finish. De Wet has been playing the game fine down in the Free State, and destroyed 2,000 bags of our mail during June, and 40,000 suits of winter clothing. I think if he were captured it would go a long way to make old Botha surrender.'

Reading this letter made me think what a soft life I have had. It also made me realise by how slender a thread our lives hang. Had Frank not survived his fever, which was probably typhoid fever, then I should not be here writing this today. Had he not survived the bullets and the guns, I should not be here.

It is thought that some 7,792 British soldiers were killed in action in the 2nd Boer War and about 6,000 Boers. In addition, thousands of native South Africans who had nothing to do with the war were also killed.

When Frank referred to the many men killed by disease, he was referring to an estimated 13,250. This number was nearly twice as many as the British that were killed in battle. Mr Burdett-Coutts MP for Westminster, who was also a correspondent for The Times, had been out to South Africa during the 2nd Boer War. He was shocked at the conditions he found out there and he reported back via his newspaper and the House of Commons:

'There were some 1,500 in field hospitals. Field hospitals had no beds, because, in theory, they follow an army on the march, so for seven weeks men ill of typhoid fever lay on the ground. But this was not the worst. The fever cases increased, but the accommodation, poor as it was, did not. The field hospital overflowed into bell tents constructed to hold six healthy men who are out in the open air all day. Into these were huddled ten typhoid patients who had to lie there day and night on the hard ground, or, when it rained, in three inches of mud.'

Symptoms of typhoid fever in adults start with a high temperature (fever) which usually increases throughout the day before falling the following morning; abdominal pain; diarrhoea; vomiting; a dry cough; headache; severe mental confusion, such as not knowing where you are or what is going on around you; a skin rash; and a feeling of being increasingly very unwell. If these symptoms are not treated then within a week the patient may also have all of the above plus a swollen abdomen and a slow heartbeat. During the third week, the symptoms of typhoid fever include: loss of appetite; weight loss; physical exhaustion; bouts of foul-smelling, yellow–green, watery diarrhoea; severe swelling of the abdomen; rapid breathing; further deterioration of the mental state, such as severe confusion, apathy and, in some cases, psychosis (where a person is unable to tell the difference between reality and their imagination). Some people in these later stages will also develop serious complications, such as internal bleeding.

Suffering in this way would be bad enough in a modern well-equipped hospital with good care and medicine, but feeling so unwell and lying on the floor of some empty house or tent often in inches of rain in the middle of winter, with nothing but a single blanket for comfort must have made the sufferer feel as though the world had forsaken you, and you might be happy to bid it farewell.

Burdett-Coutts went on to say:

'One night hundreds of men to my knowledge were lying in the worst stages of typhoid, with only a blanket and a thin waterproof sheet (not even the latter for many of them) between their aching bodies and the hard ground, with no milk and hardly any medicines, without beds, stretchers, or mattresses, without pillows, without linen of any kind, without a single nurse amongst them, with only a few ordinary private soldiers to act as 'orderlies', rough and utterly untrained to nursing, and with only three doctors to attend on 350 patients. There were none of the conditions of a forced march about this. It was a mile from Bloemfontein. There was a line of railway to two seaports, along which thousands of troops and countless trainloads of stores and equipment of all kinds, and for everyone except the sick, had been moving up during the whole of that leisurely halting time.

Besides other deficiencies which cannot be described there were no sheets or pillow-cases or pretence of bed linen of any kind; only the coarse rug grated against the sensitive skin burning with fever. The heat of these tents in the midday sun was overpowering, their odours sickening. Men lay with their faces covered with flies in black clusters, too weak to raise a hand to brush them off, trying in vain to dislodge them by painful twitching of the features. There was no one to do it for them. At night there were not enough to prevent those in the delirious stage from getting up and wandering about the camp half naked in the bitter cold. In one tent, where some slept and others lay with eyes open and staring, a case of 'perforation' was groaning out his life huddled-against his neighbour on the ground. Men had not only to see, but often to feel, others die.'

Burdett-Coutts was ridiculed by many in the House of Commons and by senior military and medical men who more or less said that this was war and you could not expect it to be run like a garden party. There was much debate as to who was more right or wrong. However, first-hand reports from another newspaper and the British Medical Journal added weight to Burdett-Coutts' account of the state of the hospitals.

The British Medical Journal printed a report from a surgeon who was at Bloemfontein which stated that when the hospital arrived at Bloemfontein, the health of the troops was bad.

'...They had been without proper tents or shelter, and the nights had often been pouring wet. The ground in many places was a swamp, and much of it had been fouled. Within a few days ....enteric fever [an alternative name for typhoid fever] broke out in many camps, and spread rapidly. It appeared to have been brought in by the men in many cases, but it is certain that in many other cases it was acquired through bad water or other local insanitary conditions......there were no general hospitals at Bloemfontein, and in spite of utilising buildings in the town the field hospitals speedily became overcrowded, so that they had to accommodate three or four times the numbers for which they were equipped, and it became impossible to nurse or treat the patients satisfactorily.....there were at that time over 5,000 sick at Bloemfontein, most of whom were suffering from enteric, while at Kroonstad three hotels, the town hall, and the churches had been converted into hospitals.

A Birmingham soldier, who had been invalided home from Bloemfontein, said that while in the hospital he frequently saw naked men in a delirious state wandering about on freezing cold nights. He had several times to wait seven or eight hours before he could get a drink of water.....he was in hospital twenty-one days he never saw a nurse. The major portion of the men had to lie on the ground. The stench in the tents was terrible. On one occasion after a thunderstorm he lay in a pool of water for almost an hour and no one came to him.

An invalid member of the Army Service Corps, who was attached to the 9th Divisional Field Hospital outside Bloemfontein, and who arrived in England June 26th, wrote to the " Daily Mail," stating that on April 3rd, when suffering from enteric, he was put into a small marquee with fifteen other men suffering from various complaints, and there lay on the ground with just one blanket under him for three weeks. He and other men had no change of garments, and were smothered with *vermin. On some days the doctor never came near them. He was finally sent down with a train-load of men to Wynberg [just outside Cape Town]. The journey took two and a half days, but rations for one day only were served out......A soldier's wife sent a letter from her sick husband at Bloemfontein, in which he stated that the sufferings of the enteric patients were horrible in the extreme. Thousands of patients were in a frightful state, even the barest necessities being unobtainable.'*

Frank's illness kept him in South Africa longer than the rest of his brigade. They left in November 1900. Presumably the army was determined to get their time out of him as he had been laid low for some time. Once recovered, he was dispatched to another brigade (G) of the Royal Horse Artillery and had to stay out there until the following May when he was ordered home because his reservist status was time expired.

The homecoming

Frank arrived back from South Africa in May 1901 on HMS Montrose. He arrived back to a country with a King not a Queen. The long reign of Victoria had ended on 22 January that year and her son Edward VII had assumed the throne, ushering in the Edwardian era.

Frank's arrival back in Wales was reported on Friday 24 May 1901 in the Carmarthenshire newspaper, The Journal. Frank, it seems, had sent a telegram to his cousin, Mary Thomas in Abergwili, to say he had arrived safely at Aldershot having landed at Southampton on Saturday 18 May. The newspaper let it be known that, *'a splendid reception is being organised for his return'.*

In fact, the celebrations continued for a few months and, as you will see, were reported in considerable detail in local newspapers in Carmarthen and Llanelli.

First, Abergwili was to have its turn.

Garlands were stretched across the street from the Sheaf Inn to Junction Cottage. There was a banner bearing, *'To our gallant defender'*, and flags waved in the breeze from almost every house in the village. At this point in the report, the journalist took the opportunity to have a go at those houses which did not, describing them as, '...*ruins which are a disgrace to Abergwili'.*

Children marched in groups singing patriotic songs as the village waited in anticipation for our hero's return.

Frank arrived at Carmarthen by train accompanied by his cousin, Mary, who had gone to Swansea to meet the London train. At the railway station they were met by a reception party from Abergwili. The party was headed by the local curate and included the schoolteacher, two neighbours of Mary Thomas, Mary's mother Esther, the superintendent of the water bailiffs with whom Frank had worked when he first came to Wales, and a journalist from Carmarthen who was to report on the magnificent homecoming.

At the station, Frank and Mary were rushed to a waiting horse-drawn waggonette bearing a large Royal ensign. As they journeyed through Carmarthen town, out along Priory Street, '...*people flocked to their doors and gave the soldier lusty cheers...*'

By the time they reached Abergwili, it was 7.15pm and the village was alive with spectators, many of whom were schoolchildren dressed in bright colours and waving flags. As the waggonette drove into the village, '...*thunderous cheers rose from the multitude...Amidst the waving of hands and loud cheering the vehicle continued its journey through the village turned round near the Palace (the Bishop's Palace) and back again to the White Ox. Here the school children were drawn up in lines and, under the control of Mr E Heard Davies, sang 'Rule Britannia' and 'Home, sweet home' very sweetly, the large concourse of people joining in the chorus.*'

The Vicar then welcomed Frank back heartily and fulsomely on behalf of the village. Gunner Lewis was said to be visibly moved and although he said he could not express in words his thanks for the very hearty and kind reception they had given him, went on to do just that in some style in the following report:

'...*He had only done his duty to his Queen, King and country, and now he was proud and happy to be among them once again. He had fared hardships and dangers, but the welcome he had received compensated him for all he suffered. On many a dreary night on the veldt and by many a camp fire his thoughts had been with them in Abergwili, and his only wish then was that he might be spared to see them all again. [cheers went up] That wish had been gratified (sic) and no one knew how thankful and pleased he was to be back among them [hear, hear]...*'

At this point, there were more cheers and then the Vicar took over once more. 'Auld lang syne' was then sung 'heartily' by the people before Mrs Davies of Llwynteg, '...*rendered 'Hen wlad fy Nhadau' in capital style, and also sang the solo of 'God save the King', in the chorus of which all joined'.* After more sonorous cheers the crowd dispersed having enjoyed a very happy gathering.

Our hero's fame spread as the Journal ran with the following article on Frank's escapades in South Africa. The style of the article is jingoistic and probably sensationalised for the benefit of the reader. It also reads as though the reporter had been round some of Frank's friends to pick up on the stories.

'Gunner Frank Lewis will not say much about the hardships he has passed through, but one or two anecdotes he has told to his friends since his arrival home give one an inkling of the sort of life he has led since he was transported from his post at Ammanford in that momentous autumn of 1899 to the battlefields of South Africa.

"Eat it!" he ejaculated, when asked about the palateableness of 'mealies' [a South African term for corn or maize], yes, and glad to get it very often. I have seen men frying it in candle grease and when that was scarce I have seen the dubbing for greasing the boots taken out of the tin, and mixed with the mealies to make a cake! And they were glad to get it too."

From such incidents as these, and the assurance that he is glad to get back to his constabulary duties, one may draw one's own conclusions.

Gunner Lewis has seen so much of the campaign from its very outset that few returned soldiers can be more interesting. Of narrow escapes he has had many. Once the order was given to mount and simultaneously he heard the scream of a shell rather "low down". Instead of mounting, Gunner Lewis "marked time" with his foot in the saddle for a few seconds, and thus probably saved his life, whereas the shell which he heard burst close over him blew off the arm of a quartermaster-sergeant who had raised his arm and was in the act of mounting.

On another occasion he saw a gun with its crew all lying down around it except one. They had all been shot except the one, who was a fellow standing six foot three in his socks.

"Sure," cried this fellow to his wounded comrades around him, working away at the gun, "they can't hit this child at all."

At that instant a bullet snapped his ankle, and he dropped without a sound.

Speaking of the destruction of the shells, Gunner Lewis says that if the Boer shells had only exploded as well as our own the loss at the beginning of the campaign would have been much greater. As to our shells he had known one of those which his brigade handled (three inches diameter) kill 32 men and wound 25.

On one occasion he saw Kruger at a distance. The ex-President was on a kopje with Steyn addressing a crowd of Boers when Lewis' detachment dropped a few shells among them. Kruger hurriedly left without even crying, "Can't stop!".

Soon after that some of our men charged a position and one of the Boers stuck to his post, firing to the last. He had just shot one man when our fellows overtook him. Thereupon the Boer threw up his arms and cried, "Me finish now; me fighting for the

Ingleeshe." But a bayonet thrust was the last he saw of the *"Ingleeshe."*

Of the Colonials [men from Canada, Australia and so on who fought with the British], Gunner Lewis speaks with admiration, although he admits they are a rough lot at times. Their idea of discipline is very different from ours, likewise their method of fighting.

"Say, lads," said the Colonel of a Colonial regiment to his men, pointing to a kopje occupied by a swarm of Boers, "our meat is up there; guess we'd better go up and take it." And they took it.

Men and officers are in many respects held among them as equal and sometimes they are ugly customers to deal with.

Once a body of Strathcona's horse were passing a Boer farm. They entered and purchased some bread from the women who gave them a very friendly greeting. When the Strathconas were leaving however, there was a volley from the farm house and several of the Canadians dropped, shot from behind. Back went the Canadians like a whirlwind and finding several armed Boers with smoking rifles there strung them up to the nearest tree.

Presently up came a well-known general of the regulars, horrified at the sight of the hanging bodies. "Here I say you inhuman scoundrels," shouted the general, "Cut those bodies down at once."

The Strathconas took no notice of the General but the latter's indignation growing, one of the Canadians quietly remarked to him, "Say there are seven bodies there now aren't there? Waal, I guess, you'd better slip away or we'll seek the eighth." And the general had to go.

Terrible fellows these Colonials, but magnificent fighters and absolutely reliable...'

In June 1901, it was the turn of Ammanford to welcome home Frank and two other soldiers. This time, the Llanelly and County Guardian reported the event. Again the tone was extravagantly patriotic bordering on jingoistic. The men were described as having done, *'...splendid service in South Africa, and have now returned home with all their blushing honours thick upon them.'*

The report went on:

'...The celebrations on Monday were of a very lavish scale, and were participated in by at least 3,000 people, all of whom displayed great enthusiasm. In addition, there was plenty of music provided in the presence of three bands, but the sonorous

notes of the bandsmen were often drowned by the din of the voices. The volunteers were present in force under Captain Roberts, and besides, the procession included about 30 horsemen and a few hundred cyclists. Altogether it was a brave show and will form a memorable event in the history of the district. The procession started from Pantyffynon, the three heroes being drawn around in a waggonette. They then proceeded to Tirdail and made a triumphal tour of the district.

Finally, a huge meeting was held in the square at Ammanford, which was densely crowded. Indeed, as one much-squeezed individual remarked, there was not room there to stuff an egg.

The enthusiastic proceedings were presided over by County Councillor W. N. Jones, who made a stirring speech, which found a response in the hearts of his listeners. Mr Jones referred, in eloquent terms, to the good work done by their three friends, and concluded by congratulating then on their safe return after having passed through such thrilling experiences.

Speeches were also delivered by Supt. J Vaughan Phillips, Capt. Roberts, Mr Iestyn Williams, Mr Ivor Morris and others.

A very graceful response was made by Gunner Lewis on behalf of his friends and himself, after which the proceedings closed.'

Guest of the Carmarthenshire Constabulary

After a couple of weeks to get used to being back with friends and family, Frank settled back into life in Carmarthenshire. He resumed his role of local constable on 15 June 1901. By then, he was boarding in Llanelli. He had also started to court his cousin Mary, who still lived with her widowed mother Esther in the White Ox in Abergwili.

Back on the beat, Frank was dealing with the usual round of characters like Elizabeth Edwards, charged with drunkenness in Murray Street in Llanelli.

'PC Francis Lewis stated that he saw the female prisoner in Murray Street. She was in a very drunken state, staggering along, singing hymns. He advised her to go home quietly, but she only became more noisy, and said that now they had locked her husband up, they might as well take her in too, and advised him to get a cab. With the assistance of a man in the crowd, she was taken into custody.

Mr Hughes [Magistrate] said, "You cannot come here and kick up dust in this way. In this case you will be fined 10s."

The Prisoner, who said the trouble was all through their lodging in a public house, was allowed time to pay.'

But, despite being back at work in the police force, Frank's homecoming parties as a soldier were not yet over.

In August, Frank was guest of honour of the Carmarthenshire Constabulary at a complimentary dinner at the Stepney Hotel in Llanelli. One of my cousins later worked in this hotel but we had no idea that our grandfather had been wined and dined in style there some 80 years before.

The Constabulary had invited along gentlemen of the press who reported the proceedings in the smallest of details, even down to recording when people laughed at the jokes and leg pulling or gave applause to welcome Frank's safe homecoming.

'...*In the unavoidable absence of Supt. Picton Phillipps, the chair was well filled by Inspector Evans* [who was based at Market Street Police Station]... *A first class spread had been provided by Hostess Lloyd, and left nothing to be desired. The post prandial proceedings were as successful as the banquet...The usual loyal toasts were first drunk most enthusiastically, Inspector Evans remarking that there were none more loyal subjects of the King than the Carmarthenshire Constabulary.*

The guest of the evening was felicitously proposed by Sergt. Michelmore, New Dock [an area of Llanelli]. *In doing so, he said that however important the toasts that had just been proposed and were going to be proposed that evening, he did not think that any of them demanded such attention as the one he was about to propose (applause). To do justice to this toast and to their guest he would ask them to bear with him in going back to the commencement of the lamentable war in which their friend had been engaged – the greatest and most redeeming feature of which was that but for the war they would not be there that evening (laughter).'*

Sergt. Michelmore having got the floor was going to make the most of his audience. He continued to give his version of the Boer War:

'*They would recollect that at the time their comrade, PC Frank Lewis, was called out, our soldiers in South Africa were in a very sad plight indeed, and the outlook appeared very gloomy. General White was boxed up in Ladysmith, while Mafeking and Kimberley were crying for relief. Upon arriving in South Africa, PC Lewis was fortunate in being attached to General French's forces, and after weeks of hard fighting, the Boer ranks were eventually pierced, and from that time success began to attend the British arms.'*

He claimed that:

'*...the joining of French's forces with those of Lewis were amply justified by results* [laughter and applause]

But, there was one illuminating fact which in fairness to their guest he must not allow to pass unnoticed. What has General French done since Lewis left him? [loud laughter].'

Warming now to his subject and pressed on by the laughter and toasting, Sergt. Michelmore continued:

'*...He had simply captured a few cattle and sheep* [continued laughter].'

He asked them to draw their own conclusions:

'*...who was responsible for the success of General French?* [laughter].'

He noticed that since their guest was unfortunately obliged to return home worn out with sickness and hardship, the Boers appeared to have taken heart again. And this was not a healthy sign that the war would end soon. He hoped that now PC Lewis had come back among them, he would be allowed to remain here for years to come [great applause].

Now, one by one, others members of the Constabulary stood up for their turn to welcome home our Frank. PC Morgan of Ferryside said he was:

'...*truly thankful that providence had spared [Frank] to return safely home...* 'and '...*trusted that his stay in the police force at Llanelly would be as successful as it had been in the South African war (great applause).*'

The Chairman of the proceedings, Inspector Evans, now took his turn, daring to compare the Egyptian Campaign (in 1882 when Britain and France sent a combined fleet to Alexandria to protect their interests) to the South African war whilst making the point that Frank's war in South Africa had been the worse of the two. He went on to say that he was:

'...*heartily glad to see him looking so well ...and...was sure if General French needed Lewis' services any more he would be only too ready to go out again (loud applause).*'

Having said that, Inspector Evans said he hoped that they would not lose him again and that he would be allowed to remain in Llanelly to fight their little battles.

After the Chairman came PC John Rees who was the person who had seen service in Egypt. He gladly agreed that compared with the South African war his time in Egypt had been nothing. Constable Rees said that all the time Frank was out in South Africa they had looked every morning at the casualty lists and happily for them they did not see Franks' name included. He hoped, to more loud applause, that no occasion would arise again to call one of them away from Llanelly.

Then it was the turn of PC Britten from Llandeilo to support the toast and to add his remarks. He had been with Frank the night before he had been called away. He recalled that Frank had appeared to be very glad to have the chance to fight for his Queen and country. To more applause, he wished him every success from the bottom of his heart.

The toasts were by now being enthusiastically drunk with musical honours as accompaniment.

It was then Frank's turn to rise and respond. He was greatly moved (and, by now, probably quite drunk) by the evening's proceedings, and said that he felt very glad and greatly honoured with the reception that they had given him that night. When he said that it was more than he expected and more than he deserved, he was shouted down with cries of, 'No, no!' He said he could hardly express how glad he was to be back amongst them again. He told them that his thoughts had often wandered back to the happy times he spent in the force while he was out in South Africa.

It was clear from the tales he told his eager listeners, that when he went out to South Africa he had not expected to be there long. Indeed, he and his soldier companions had thought they were in for a nice sea journey and the war might be over before they landed. Frank held his audience spellbound with a graphic account of his exploits whilst attached to General French's forces: tales of Kimberley, Mafeking and the terrible battle at Paardeberg. In the latter campaign, their convoy had been captured and they went from the Saturday to the following Tuesday without anything to eat, and had little or no water to drink for two days. He told how the Boers in their retreat had set fire to the veldt leaving several of Frank's wounded comrades to be burned to death.

As the evening wore on, and the drink took further hold, the Chairman began a series of speeches and toasts to their senior officers, starting with the Chief Constable, who, '...had done more to bring evil doers to justice single-handed than any other Chief Constable in the United Kingdom...'. Furthermore, he was, '...equal to any four policemen in...England, Scotland, or Wales...'. As the eulogy continued, it transpired that the Chief Constable had often been seen going into a shop in Llanelly to buy something to send to Frank at the front. Many of these presents, and some very useful ones were sent out, he was sorry to say never reached their guest but got into the hands of the Boers.

Given this fine start there was then a queue of officers all of whom stood up and spoke in the highest praise of Chief Constable Phillipps. Having done the Chief Constable proud, the toasts then moved on to the Superintendents, according to PC Morgan, who had worked with the Gloucestershire and Glamorganshire Constabularies before coming further west, '...*a better class of superintendents could never be found than in the Carmarthenshire Constabulary...at all times only too ready to support and advise the men under their charge...*'. With that another toast was proposed, '...*let them continue to be loyal and true to their superior officers and success was assured...*' and seconded to great applause.

By now there was much singing ably led by a sergeant and some of his constables. The evening was rounded off by more toasts this time to the gentlemen of the Press whose good copy by now was secure, and to Miss Lloyd, mine hostess.

At this stage, I think that carriages would have been called to make sure that all members of the party were taken safely home.

Something to cheer up a November day

'The explosion of fog-signals, the continuous report of cannonettes and other fire arms, a splendid display of bunting, including garlands of flags stretched across the street, warned the visitor that some unusual occurrence was about to take place in Abergwili on Wednesday morning', so reported The Journal on Friday 22 November 1901.

It was the wedding day of Miss Mary Thomas, only daughter of Mrs Esther Thomas, White Ox Inn – *'a young lady of great popularity throughout the district – and Mr Frank Lewis grandson of the late Mr W Lewis, Penygraig Abergwili, a constable stationed at Llanelly, and reservist who had recently returned from active service in South Africa, where he had served with distinction in the 'Chestnut troop'* [the name given to A battery of the RHA] *of the RHA under General French in his celebrated march from Kimberly to Pretoria Martial accompaniment was therefore very appropriate'.*

It is interesting that Frank is described as the grandson of his grandfather, William, rather than son of his father, Francis, who after all was a son of Abergwili. Perhaps this is something of a clue that Francis left Abergwili as a bit of a black sheep. Or it could just be that the family disapproved of the fact that he had left at all. But maybe it was because of the shame of Francis having died in the workhouse.

Frank and Mary's wedding took place in the parish church in Abergwili, *'…packed with well-wishers from far and near and included many of the local landed gentry'.*

The Journal gave an account of the wedding which was a bit like Hello magazine without the pictures. First there was a detailed description of the bridegroom (*'…every inch a soldier in his khaki uniform…'*) and his bride (*'…very pretty in a handsome grey cashmere dress, trimmed with white silk chiffon plass menteri… grey toque trimmed with orange blossom and ostrich feathers… gold curb bangle and a gold Kruger locket, the gift of the bridegroom… a choice bouquet of exotic flowers, the gift of Mr Turberville'* [gardener at the Bishop's Palace in Abergwili]). I struggled to know what plass menteri was and can only conclude that the journalist did too and it was meant to be 'passementerie' a decorative textile trimming consisting of gold or silver lace, gimp, or braid.

Then there were the bridesmaids, Miss Mary Lewis, cousin, of Parkyricks and Miss Kate Jones of Grove Cottage. The former, *'...attired in a white cashmere dress, with large white hat to match, and the latter wore a petunia coloured cloth dress trimmed with white silk, her hat being a black picturesque one. Both wore gold safties, the gift of the bridegroom...'* After much research, I still do not know what these gold items were that the bridegroom had given to the bridesmaids but presumably he brought them back from South Africa along with the Kruger gold locket and curb bangle given to the bride.

The best man, resplendent in his morning suit and bowler hat, was PC Britten from Ammanford, a close friend of the groom for as long as Frank had been in the police force.

The ceremony was delivered by the curate and the Vicar, both conveniently called Reverend Thomas. They alluded to the service given by the groom to his country and to the high esteem in which the bride was held. The choir (of which the bride was a faithful member) sang an 'appropriate' hymn. The bride was given away by her uncle, Mr James Davies, The Elms Gowerton. According to the 1901 census, James Davies was a police inspector. I have never managed to work out exactly how someone called James Davies could be her uncle. She did have an uncle called James, her mother Esther's younger brother. But surely he would have been a Lewis? And in any case that James Lewis disappears from view between the 1861 and 1871 census leaving me thinking he had died.

If James Davies had been one of her father's brothers then he would have been a Thomas. This is a mystery and the nearest I can get to it is by thinking that he was the husband of one of the sisters of Esther or John Thomas (Mary's father).

But I digress.

Back at the wedding, we learn that amongst the guests are: the schoolmaster and choirmaster, Mr Evan Heard Thomas, and his daughters, May and Poppie (who presided at the organ); Lewis the local coal merchant; Stokes the journalist, son of an Irish retired soldier; Jones the coffee tavern; Lewis the Falcon Inn in Carmarthen, one of the oldest inns in town; Evans the tailor and draper from Swansea; and Superintendent J Evans.

The couple left the church to a fine rendering of Mendelsohn's Wedding March and were greeted outside with showers of rice and confetti. They then proceeded along the High Street to the White Ox where the table had been beautifully laid out for the wedding breakfast. Here we know that the bride and groom were the recipients of, '...*a large number of useful and in many cases very costly presents*'. No doubt this qualified comment had some wondering when they read the account in the paper if their gift was thus described!

After the reception, at which speeches and toasts were warmly received and ably responded to, the couple left on the train for Swansea, '...*where among with other places, the honeymoon will be spent*'. We are never told the names of the other places.

Several photographs of the wedding day have survived. When I first saw them and thought that these were my grandparents, I was shocked. There they stood from a different era which of course they were: Victorians becoming Edwardians. I thought of friends from school who had their grandmothers living with them when we were teenagers and of other friends who went to visit their grandparents for Sunday dinner or to pick up a cardigan the grandmother had knitted for them. Here were my grandparents from another era, dead long before I was even born.

I also thought that Frank must have borrowed someone else's army uniform because it did not look like anything that I had seen before. His jacket had upside down stripes or chevrons on the bottom of the cuffs, but what I did not know was that these were clues to his military service.

Originally introduced in 1836, these good conduct chevrons were awarded to those below the rank of Sergeant, and were worn on the right lower sleeve. In 1881 this was changed to the left lower sleeve. A man wearing them also received the relevant good conduct pay. Because they were for good conduct and the man received a gratuity, they could also be forfeited for misconduct and had to be re-earned. The fact that

Frank's jacket bears three of these shows that he had served for 12 years with good conduct.

I thought that the hat looked a bit colonial – maybe Australian or Canadian, but I am told that these were regular wear by the end of the Boer War.

Frank and Mary pictured standing outside the White Ox in Abergwili. Mary's face seems to have been touched up in the photo no doubt because of the veil shading her features.

The picture below is of (left to right standing): Kate Jones, bridesmaid; PC Britten, best man; Frank and Mary, the happy but somewhat solemn couple; and Mary Lewis, cousin and bridesmaid. Seated are: on the right, Esther Thomas, the bride's mother and the groom's aunt, and, on the left, probably James Davies the uncle who gave Mary Thomas away.

Looking at Esther, I thought she must be at least in her 80s but born in 1838 she would have been 63 that year. Today, at that age, she might have been going to keep fit, babysitting for her grandchildren or still working full time. Here she seems to have settled into a sedentary life modelling herself on Queen Victoria for her remaining days. James is only 55, but

he, too, looks much older. Given what we know of Frank's height, around five feet ten inches, this photograph shows Mary, at the age of 24, as very tiny indeed, little more than five feet tall, if that.

Raising a family

During the next eighteen years, Mary gave birth to seven children: three boys and four girls. One of the boys and one of the girls died in infancy. The boy died aged 5 months from infantile diarrhoea and exhaustion. The girl died aged 10 months from fits associated with teething. I look at this information and it seems incredible that a child could die from teething, or for that matter from diarrhoea. Yet even up to the first half of the 20th century, it was a common occurrence for parents to suffer the loss of one or more children in infancy from what are now minor ailments.

Mary Valentine and William Francis Lewis:note the Kruger locket around Mary's neck.

Mary's waist in the photograph must be a miracle of corsetry. See the advertisement taken from a newspaper advertisement of the time (Llanelly and County Guardian) and you can understand why! With the aid of such items of torture, the wearer could achieve a 16 to 18 inch waist and probably considerable discomfort to the abdomen and chest into the bargain.

The first five of Frank and Mary's children, including the two who did not survive, were born in Llandebie. The family lived for some of the time on the outskirts of Llandebie in one of two wooden houses built on Ammanford Road. There are still two such houses next to one another by the river. The houses look incongruous in this small West Wales village, being American in design, complete with a wooden roofed porch or verandah. It seems that a local man had gone out to Cleveland, Ohio in America, for some time before returning home. The only houses he knew how to build were the type he had put up out in America. I don't know if Frank named the house, or if the name was what drew him to it, but it was called Kimberley Villa.

The names given to Frank and Mary's children were of great fascination to me as a child. I had been given only one name at birth and felt somewhat short-changed. I was slightly envious that my father's generation were, all but one, given three Christian names. And what names! They were: John Francis <u>Denton</u>; William James Leslie (the boy who died in infancy); <u>Kenneth</u> Arthur Leslie (my father – who hated the name Leslie and always signed his name K. A. Lewis); <u>Hetty</u> Louisa Maud (the girl who died in infancy); Mary <u>Isabel</u>; <u>Violet</u> Margaret Brittannia (spelled as shown!); and <u>Primrose</u> <u>Vera</u> <u>Jenny</u>. The underlined names show how they were known. I have underlined all of PVJ's names as I have known her be called each of them throughout her life. Seemingly in opposition to the mouthful that was her name, Violet Margaret Brittannia was satisfied with just Vi and, outside the family, my father was more often than not known as Ken.

The two brothers Denton and Kenneth played together and often argued. One day, out in the garden of Kimberley Villa, Kenneth teased his older brother with his favourite soft toy. He kept pushing the stuffed elephant with red and gold trimmings at Denton who kept backing away. Eventually, Denton fell backwards and into the river which flowed at the bottom of the garden. Fortunately for both boys in different ways, the woman next door was cleaning her windows and saw what had happened. She and the boys' mother together pulled out Denton crying and spouting water from the river. Later, Kenneth was soundly trounced and shut away with the loss of the offending toy. Whether this incident was the basis for it or not, my father and his brother never were the best of friends.

Kenneth aged about 2 years old –
before his first proper hair cut.

It was whilst the family lived in Llandebie that Frank became a bit of a local hero. An Act of Parliament had long been passed that forbade the payment of workers in the truck tokens or 'Tommy tickets' that we saw in Witton Park. The truck system was a factory management device which ensured that workers spent at least some of their wages in the shops owned by the bosses. In many cases, the goods were inferior yet the prices were high. Many of these shops also gave credit, encouraging people to run up debts. The dangers and unfairness of the arrangement had long been recognised. In fact, the truck system had been illegal since 1831. Despite that, it carried on for many years in Wales and elsewhere especially in the coalfields and iron mining districts of South Wales. The passing of the Truck Amendment

Act of 1887 was meant to get rid of the practice once and for all. This news seems to have bypassed Llandebie as the 110 or so workers in the local lime burning works were still paid half in cash and half in meat, bacon and groceries from the factory shop.

One Saturday, a committee of workers came to see Frank at his home. They complained bitterly about the sharp practice still carried on in the works. Things had reached a climax on the day when the workers or their wives were told that there was no fresh meat for them, only salty, fatty bacon which they could take or leave. On the workers' behalf, PC Frank Lewis went along to the manager and the cashier and pointed out that what they were doing was against the law. The works' managers as good as told Frank that they could do as they pleased. Frank did not argue but just informed them that he would issue them with a summons for breaching the law. The managers were forced to attend the Magistrates' Court in Llanelli where they had to answer 110 charges, one for each man employed at the works. On appearing in court the manager and the cashier each received a fine with costs and cautioned that any further breach would result in heavier fines and costs. Leaving the court, the manager came face to face with Frank and said, '...*Lewis, there's a bloody comic you are!*'

Moving on

After the spell in Llandebie the family's next stop, on 20 November 1909, was Pwll, a small coastal village just to the west of Llanelli. The village was home to a majority of locally born people, most of them bilingual (Welsh and English). Surnames like, Hughes, Samuel, Williams, Evans, Jones and Morgan left you in no doubt where you were. The main employers in the village were a local coal mine and the nearby tinworks.

Amongst this Welsh community had blown in several families from other parts of the United Kingdom. There was James McKenrick from Newcastle-upon-Tyne, a shaft sinker in the colliery with his family and children. His wife and three of his children were from Northumberland, but you could see that they had travelled backwards and forwards from the North East, stopping en route as their 13 year old had been born in Sheffield. The family had boarders, three married men away from their families. One was James' boss – Walter Maurice Redfearn, whose wife was living up in Whitley Bay with her widowed mother. Another was an Irishman from Cork and the third from Derbyshire. Herbert Kitchin, a bricklayer from Chelsea and his wife and daughter from London had settled in the village, taking in a gasfitter from Hereford to help pay the rent. A housepainter all the way from Scotland with his wife from Manchester was clearly a wanderer whose children's places of birth (Llandudno, Wigan and Pembrey) traced some of his travels. Another Scotsman, James Martin, also a pit sinker, had brought his family here too. On the outskirts of the village, at the end nearest to Llanelli, lived a butler from Shropshire, a coachman in gentleman's service, and two brothers (gardeners from Gloucester) in domestic service in part of the Stradey estate.

The village was well supplied with tradesmen and women: a tailor, several dressmakers, dairymen and dairymaids, publicans, people working for a mineral water maker, fruit hauliers and a florist. There were several teachers, too including Thomas Isaac, Rachel Lloyd and the 18 year old

Mary Powell. We will hear more, in due course, of the most senior of these schoolteachers, William Henry Hughes.

There is no doubt that Frank's Welsh, learned originally in the North East courtesy of his father, would have improved living in Pwll. So many people he encountered day-to-day would speak only Welsh. At home, his wife spoke both languages to their children. Apart from the one year old Isabel, he and his family are described on the 1911 census as being able to speak both Welsh and English.

Frank, Mary and their children lived in the Police Station, quite a large place for a growing family. Life here was relatively quiet. But much to his embarrassment, one thing that Frank had to sort out involved his own sons, Denton and Kenneth, and a piece of police equipment.

In 1910, the 7 and 5 year olds and their mates were playing on the big bank known as the Graig at the front of their house in New Road, Pwll. The bank was covered in dry bracken. The Lewis boys went out to play, taking with them their father's police lamp. At the front of the lamp was a highly-magnifying glass. Off they went to the thickest and driest part of the Graig and started to use the magnifying glass to focus the sun on some very dry fern so as to set it alight. Very soon they had a lovely fire blazing. The boys whooped with delight and danced around the fire pretending to be American Indians. But, when they tired of this entertainment, they found they could not put out the fire which by now was spreading rapidly across the Graig. The boys ran for help and Frank along with several other men from the village came up the hill with wet sacks to try to extinguish the fire which by now had got a firm hold. It took many hours and dashes up and down the hill to put out the fire. Later that night there was the inquest. Having considered everything, the men came to the conclusion that a broken bottle must have acted like a magnifying glass for the sun's rays. That might have been the end of the matter had it not been for one member of the gang who began to boast about how the fire had really happened. Before long there had been another bush fire – of information that got back to Frank. The Lewis brothers both experienced another piece of police equipment, the belt from their father's police overcoat.

Kenneth (seated) and Denton aged about 5 and 7 respectively.

The brothers were fortunate that their doting grandmother (Esther) was staying with them at the time as she intervened to stop the punishment which otherwise looked set to continue for some time.

The two Lewis boys went to the small village school when they lived in Pwll. Kenneth was in the class taken by our Mr Hughes of previous mention. By Kenneth's account, Mr Hughes was a man of a very mean disposition. He maintained what he called 'discipline' through the ready use of the cane. To make matters worse, he would single out one of the boys to go to a nearby wooded copse and cut new sticks suitable for use as canes. As you might imagine, this was not a popular job. One particular day, Mr Hughes chose Kenneth to search for the canes. Reluctantly, Kenneth had to go. Having chosen the sticks, Kenneth began to make his way back to school across a field where cows were grazing. Choosing a freshly dropped cowpat, he then poked the ends of the sticks therein. He waited a few moments for the stuff to dry and headed back to the classroom. Now Mr Hughes had a habit of picking his teeth with the ends of the canes. The next lesson he did just so. How the boys laughed to see him spluttering and spitting. He realised what Kenneth had done but could not prove it. This incident was a turning point and a good result for the boys as he never sent any of them for canes ever again.

In 1910, Frank would have read about something in the newspaper that would have made him think back to his army days and the journey back from South Africa. On 21 July that year following the murder of his wife, one Hawley Harvey Crippen fled London for Brussels with his mistress Ethel La Neve. Soon after, with his mistress disguised as a boy, they boarded HMS Montrose in Antwerp. Although rebuilt twice in the intervening period, HMS Montrose was the same ship that had brought Frank home from the Boer War in 1901. As a policeman and lover of murder mysteries, Frank would have been keen to read the grisly story which captured the interest of the country that summer. The court heard that Crippen had poisoned his wife, cut up and buried some of the remains in the cellar. The head and larger bones were never found.

Crippen was the first person to be apprehended with the aid of the newly developed Marconi radio wireless. Crippen was hanged later that year. Nearly a century later, DNA testing of tissue samples of the victim and her living female descendants seems to cast doubt on whether the remains in the cellar were those of Cora, Crippen's wife.

Frank would have loved the continuing mystery.

1911: a year to remember

In early 1911, the children lost their ally. Their grandmother died on 18 February 1911. She was 73 years of age although her death certificate says she was only 68. Like her father William Lewis, Esther seemed to have a propensity for losing a few years along the way. Esther died of

senile decay, what nowadays we would call dementia, and syncope, an old term for losing consciousness. I guess in the end we all lose consciousness so this term was not particularly informative.

Esther Thomas in her late 60s/early 70s

Esther was laid out in the front room of the house in New Road, Pwll. Six years old at the time, my father remembered being taken into the room to see her in her coffin. The cloying sweet smells of the perfume used by the undertaker and the white lilies in the room where she lay for family and friends to pay their last respects were things he could conjure up every time he saw a funeral.

The elderly matriarch went to her resting place in Abergwili churchyard in some style by all accounts. The funeral cortege took hours to make its slow journey of nearly 20 miles led by a horse-drawn black carriage bearing her ornate coffin. My father went to the funeral dressed in a specially-made black suit. His most profound memory of the day was that the hearse was pulled by four black horses and they had to stop at

Llandefaelog Hill at the half way point to Abergwili for a fresh set of horses plus another two to help pull the carriage up the steep hill and for the remainder of the journey.

In the Lewis family, the death of Esther seemed like the end of an era. On the national stage, it was the end of the Edwardian era. A few months later, on 22 June 1911, George V was crowned King. His father Edward VII had died on Frank's 41st birthday, 6 May, the previous year.

The Coronation in Westminster Abbey took place in a heat wave that stayed with Britain from May until September that year. The summer of 1911 became known as the hottest, driest and sunniest for over 80 years and it stayed in this position until the summer of 1976. The British are not particularly good at coping with the heat at home and it was certainly the case in 1911, a fact that was to have a bearing on what happened nearer home that summer.

To set the scene further, it is useful to reflect for a moment on what life was like in Britain in the early part of the 20th century. It was a time when about a third of working adult males were paid wages of less than twenty five shillings a week for which they had to work about twelve hours a day, six days a week. That sum would have roughly the same buying power as about £70 a week today. Whilst wages had remained the same for over ten years, the cost of living had risen by 12½%. It was also a time when a privileged 1% of the population owned 60% of the country. Rather like a hundred years on, the lives of the rich and famous were of endless fascination to others. Knowledge of the lives of those who had luxuries, land and a life of excess was leading to more and more envy and discontent by the working classes. Those with little, whose daily concerns were the bare necessities of life, food, shelter and clothing, became less and less willing to sit back and accept their lot in life. Throughout that long hot summer there was increasing industrial unrest as the great divide between the rich and the poor, the privileged and the disadvantaged became more and more apparent.

The arrival of the motor car started to give freedom to those wealthy enough to own one. Moving pictures were becoming popular entertainment and by 1911 there were three cinemas in Llanelli, each with two shows in the evenings and matinees on Saturday afternoons.

Film brought national events like the Coronation and sporting events direct to the masses at admission prices of as little as two old pennies (2d). Women were increasingly becoming more aggressive in their fight for rights in a society that had not yet granted them the vote.

By the end of July, the hot summer of 1911 in Pwll and Llanelli was about to become a time that would be remembered for a very long time for very sad reasons by many in the locality.

First, there was a colliery disaster in Crown Colliery, Pwll, that resulted in the deaths of four men and in four others being seriously injured. The colliery was owned by Mr Evan Jones from Penmount in Llanelli. He had employed a firm from Newcastle-upon-Tyne, Messrs Redfearn and Co, to establish sinking operations. Nine employees of Redfearn's were bricking out the 85 yard deep shaft that had been put in. Bricklayers were working from the bottom up. They had worked up about 12 feet when a pump that was bringing out the water from the base of the shaft suddenly broke free from its ropes and crashed down killing and injuring workers on the way. Mr Redfearn who was at his nearby office rushed to the pit head to see what had happened. James McKenrick, the master sinker, had only just come up from the shaft a minute or so before the accident. He and a colleague went straight back down only to find the staging on which the men were standing had been carried down with the men as the pump hit it. They had the awful task of finding the dead and the injured.

And bigger trouble was brewing during August in nearby Llanelli that would also have the gravest of consequences for yet more families. Railwaymen went on strike nationally in protest at their wages. At that time, railwaymen were amongst the poorest paid of workers. These men were paid around £1 per week, about 20% below the norm for skilled manual workers.

The strike took place at a time that became known as the 'Great Unrest' when men and women held strikes in different industries and different parts of the United Kingdom because of poor pay and conditions. Coal workers, dock workers, seamen, carters and jam makers were just a diverse few of those who came out on strike between 1910 and 1914 for better treatment by their employers. But the news that the unrest had spread to the normally peaceable railway workers was greeted with fear and concern by politicians. The strike reaching the railwaymen was of great political and economic significance as the railways were the main means by which people (including troops), food, goods and livestock were moved about the country. If the railways ceased to run then people would soon run short of food. Discontent and disorder on a vast scale would surely follow.

The strike took hold in Llanelli on the afternoon of Thursday 17 August 1911. Taking the authorities by surprise, the 500 or so men who were employed on the railways in the area blockaded Llanelli's two level crossings that guarded the eastern and western approaches to the railway station.

The blockade was particularly politically-sensitive, as the Great Western Railway line through Carmarthenshire was the main route for troops to be shipped to and from the troubled provinces of Ireland. The crowd of railway workers grew in size to many thousands as local colliers and tinplate workers, who enjoyed comparatively generous wages, joined the strikers to show solidarity. The crowd gathered at the railway crossing gates by the station and stopped trains from passing.

To everyone's surprise, Llanelli had become the front line. That nobody had expected this is shown by the fact that about two thirds of the local police force were out of town; they had been sent to Tonypandy and Cardiff where trouble was expected with strikers. One of only eighteen policemen left in the town was Sergeant William Britten, best man at Frank and Mary's wedding. Sergeant Britten was well liked in the town and the crowd had sung, 'For he's a jolly good fellow' as he arrived early on to police the crowd that had gathered. The numbers of police were not enough to clear the protesters so they had settled down to keep the peace through a benign 'wait and see' approach, enjoying with the strikers the entertainment of impromptu mock election speeches, singing and tap dancing. Stranded rail travellers came to listen to the entertainment and the leader of the strike even offered to find free accommodation for any women and children passengers.

In the early hours of the next morning, the police tried to charge the thinning crowd but were unsuccessful. Nevertheless through negotiation with the crowd, a mail train was allowed through as it was a cattle train from Ireland. The police had pleaded to save the animals from suffering even longer in the trucks after that hot summer night.

Also early on Friday, Thomas Jones, a wholesale provision merchant, local councillor, magistrate, landowner and shareholder in the Great Western Railway was rung at home and asked to come to the railway station. When he arrived, he found that the military were expected soon. Afterwards, some would say that Thomas Jones himself had rung requesting the military intervention. Army regiments had been stationed relatively near to Cardiff, in order to quell numerous industrial flashpoints in South East Wales during this period. Soon, over a hundred soldiers of the Lancashire Regiment had arrived. They were experienced in dealing with striking miners and at first they kept the peace with little trouble. At the request of the Chief Constable, the Llanelli policemen deployed in Cardiff and Tonypandy were also soon on their way back.

Thomas Jones tried to talk to the crowd who, believing he was trying to read the Riot Act, shouted him down. Later that morning, Thomas Jones and a fellow magistrate sent a telegram to the Home Office requesting more help, saying erroneously that there were only eight policemen in town. As a result of Thomas Jones' request, more troops were called in: the Worcestershire Regiment and the Devon Regiment. Some 250 men from the regiments arrived around 6.00pm.

By Saturday morning, the Chief Constable had arrived and sent a telegram to the Home Office saying, '...*Think situation is now in hand with the assistance of the troops*'. But later that afternoon, things turned ugly. There were many and contradictory accounts of what happened but what is certain is that the officer in charge of the troops ordered a magistrate to read the Riot Act. The crowd having been warned, the officer then gave the order to fire. Shots rang out and within moments two men were dead. One was a local tin plate worker and promising rugby player who had turned up to support the railwaymen. The other, a young Londoner, was staying in Llanelli while he recuperated from tuberculosis. He had simply come out into the garden in the middle of shaving to see what all the noise was about.

Now the crowd had an even bigger grievance. The riot that broke out saw railway trucks full of goods looted and destroyed. Word spread and trucks and vans were raided in the railway sidings. All manner of goods and provisions were looted. The troops were nowhere to be seen, seemingly paralysed into inaction by earlier events. The station and railway trucks were all damaged extensively.

Before things were brought under control, four more people were killed as a result of an explosion that occurred when rioters set fire to a railway truck unaware that it contained explosive detonators. Tensions grew in the August heat. The crowd, fuelled by outrage and anger, moved into town. They attacked the Town Hall and went on to Market Street where they damaged and looted many shops. The business premises of Thomas Jones, the wholesale provision merchant, were targeted and received considerable damage.

Where was Frank when all this was going on? Well, the short and truthful answer is I do not know. But I suspect he was one of the policemen sent to Tonypandy or Cardiff as the riots were never referred to in the family. Also, it would have been unlikely that the railway strike would affect Pwll and so probably he was viewed as being temporarily redeployable.

In the wake of the events of that August, the local press was not slow to give voice to the lack of police protection that the town had felt during the strike and the subsequent riot. The Llanelly and County Guardian made its point plainly, '...*we trust that the town will not again be left absolutely unprotected...We do not pay police rates for the purpose of taking care of Tonypandy or for inculcating respect for the majesty of the law on the part of the dusky gentry of Cardiff... Indeed if the whole of the Llanelly force had been on duty on that memorable Friday, ...we might have been spared the subsequent disturbances.*'

A letter in the Llanelly Star asked, '...*What earthly good is a Chief Constable and an elaborate staff hidden away in truly rural Llandeilo with a population of about three men and a dog?...*'

The wider family

Frank's life was becoming more and more Welsh, but he was the only one of his generation who had left the North East of England. So what was happening to his sisters who had stayed in the North East?

His eldest sister Mary (known as Polly to the family) and her blacksmith husband Robert Foster had gradually made their way northwards from Teesside where they had married in Middlesbrough in 1879. Tracking the movements of the family proved tricky as the enumerator made errors in the various census returns. They became Forsters on a few records and their ages and places of birth were misreported. If their standard of literacy was limited, they would not know whether or not things had been properly recorded until 1911 when the head of the family first filled in the record.

By the start of the 20th century, Robert and Mary were living on Tyneside, first in Blaydon and then, further east, in Derwenthaugh, south of the Tyne in Gateshead. Robert seemed to be moving incrementally back towards his birthplace of Northumberland. By 1911, Mary had given birth to ten children. Seven had survived and ranged in ages from 28 to 10 years. The Lewis family Christian names were passed on to the children: William, Rachel, Isabel, Margaret and Alice along with those named after their father's side, Robert and Charles. The names were going on into the next generation too as a seven year old grandchild called Francis (Goymer) was living with the family in 1911. Francis was actually Frances Alice the eldest daughter of Rachel Foster and her husband Fred Goymer. Fred, born in Suffolk, was another migrant into the North East, a coal miner who had boarded with Rachel's parents when he came looking for work in Blaydon ten years before.

Rachel, Frank's next eldest sister, had left home early. By the age of 16, she was a domestic servant in Middlesbrough. In April 1891, aged 26, she was living in as general servant to a Scottish foreman stevedore, Charles Macauley, his wife Elizabeth and their two small children. There was also a nurse in the household, 14 year old Lily Graham. Rachel's work as a general servant, or maid of all work, would have been hard going. She would have been expected to do washing, starching and ironing when such things took days depending on the weather. She would do all the general housework such as cleaning floors and furniture in all of the rooms. In springtime, there would be a major clean of the whole house. We forget just how difficult places would be to keep clean in the days of coal fires and in an urban environment with heavy industry constantly churning out dirt and smoke.

It may have been with some relief that later in 1891, Rachel could give up her servant's duties in a stranger's home. On 27th August that year, she married a Danish seaman called Peter Benson. Her mother, Isabella, and her step father Caleb Burgess were the witnesses to their marriage in the Wesleyan Methodist Chapel in Eston. Her mother signed her name with a cross (X).

Rachel probably continued working as she had done, but now as a servant in her own home in a very industrial part of Middlesbrough. She gave birth to seven children but by 1911, as in her elder sister's family, three had died. John Alfred (18), known as Jack, the eldest of Rachel and Peter's family, had left home. He was working as a bricklayer down in Wales and lodging with his Uncle Frank's family. Lillian Maud (16), Isabella (14) and William Francis (12), the other three children of Rachel and Peter, were living at home in Oliver Street, South Bank in Middlesbrough. Peter was a ship's steward at the time he and Rachel married in 1891, but in 1911 he was a stationary engineman in a blast furnace, no longer going away to sea.

On Christmas Day 1917, Rachel was widowed. Peter's effects were worth £278.13s.2d when administration was granted to Rachel in March the following year. This sum of money was rapidly losing its buying power as World War I took its toll. By 1920, his legacy would have been worth about half what it would have been at the time of his death. Interestingly, by the time Rachel died in October 1939, aged 75, she left her eldest son £604.18s to share amongst the family. This would have had the buying power of about £17,000 nowadays. It seems she was a very canny manager of money, able to make more along the way. She had certainly moved up in the world by the time she died. In 1939, she was no longer living in an unmade street or a road overshadowed by factory, furnace, or iron mills, but in a pleasant suburban avenue: 33 Briermede Avenue, Low Fell, in Gateshead. The tidy little half-brick half-pebbledash semi-detached house with gardens front and rear was a world away from the mill noise of Hope Street in Hartlepool or the grime of the iron works in Witton Park. The house was just off the Durham Road and near to 55 acres of landscaped gardens and woodlands, a park that was on land purchased from one of the country's greatest Victorian stained glass window designers. Nearly 60 years later, people would flock to the area from all over the world to see the nearby 'Angel of the North'.

Margaret, the sister next youngest in age to Frank, had married in 1894 another man of Danish origin, another seaman. Frederick Sengelow was in the merchant service. Margaret and Frederick lived in Hartlepool and no doubt Margaret was alone for long periods of time. However, she had four children to keep her busy: Harold, Frederick, Alice and Isobel. The boys were named after Frederick and his brother and the girls were named after Margaret's younger sister and her mother.

In 1909, Frederick was left to bring up the children when Margaret died of acute gastritis and inanition (an old term for exhaustion due to lack of nourishment). She was only 38 years of age. Frederick left his life at sea and became a furnace man in the shipyard. Two years after his mother died, the eldest son, Harold, left home. At the age of 15, he joined hundreds of other similar-aged boys from all over the UK at the Royal Naval Training Establishment in Shotley near Ipswich. Frederick (aged 14), the second son, was working as an errand boy at a boot shop. The two girls (aged 12 and 11) were at school, but no doubt ran the home.

Across the Tees in Middlesbrough was Alice Esther, the youngest of Frank's sisters. Alice was described as strikingly beautiful. She worked as a lady's maid, probably to one of the wives of a successful businessman in the area. In the hierarchy of the house's servants, the lady's maid was second in seniority on the female servants' side, next in line to the housekeeper. She would have been referred to by her surname. Her duties would have included dressing her lady, helping her with make-up, hairdressing and securing jewellery. She would also have mended her lady's clothes as necessary, done shopping and cleaned her mistress' room.

In the summer of 1906, Alice Esther Lewis married John Watson Turner in the registry office in Middlesbrough. Her elder sister Rachel Benson was one of the witnesses. John Turner was a traffic foreman in the steelworks in Middlesbrough, by all accounts a well-respected man in his neighbourhood. I have seen mention of a John Turner in the Grangetown district who was the President of the local football team in 1910 when the team was a member of the Northern League. I suspect that this must be him as the only people living in Grangetown named John Turner at the time of the 1911 census were John Watson Turner and his son John Lewis Turner. At the time of the marriage, John lived at 2 Bolckow Road.

Most of the 5,000 or more inhabitants of Grangetown lived between Bolckow Road and the steel works. The Turners continued to live in Grangetown, Middlesbrough. By 1911, they had moved to 57 Granville Road, Grangetown.

Using satellite technology to view Granville Road from the confines of my computer, I find that this street still exists but has no houses, just grassed areas where the buildings had once been. The houses were by some accounts quite desirable residences as they had three bedrooms, a bathroom and that indicator of increased social standing, the inside lavatory. By the beginning of April 1911, Alice and John had three children: John Lewis Turner aged 2, Mary Isabella aged 1, and a week old child as yet unnamed. Also living with the family was an 8 year old nephew, Francis Turner. It seems that in filling in the census return, John Watson was rather creative with this last detail. The child was actually Francis Lewis, born to Alice in 1902 before she married, the result of a brief encounter with a man rumoured to be an Italian (?) or French (?) sailor. Francis was born in Hartlepool. I suspect that Alice went to live with her sister Margaret whilst she had the child. Of all of the sisters, Alice and her husband seem to have prospered more than any of them judging by the sum that John left Alice in his will when he died in 1930. The sum of £1967.7s1d would have had the modern day buying power of over £65,000. Alice lived to the ripe old age of 88. She died of bronchopneumonia in 1964.

Although only one of Frank's sisters' children carried on the Lewis name, albeit as a Christian name, Welsh genes had well and truly infiltrated the North East for generations to come on at least 19 different fronts.

Tinopolis!

Back in Wales, by December 1911, Frank's wife, Mary Lewis, had given birth to another daughter (the gloriously-named Violet Margaret Brittannia). Frank and Mary now had four surviving children – two boys aged 8 and 6 and two girls aged 2 and newly born.

Six months later, on 15 April 1912, ominously the same day that Titanic sank, Frank, Mary and the children were on the move again. This time they were off to Llanelli. Frank had swapped places with PC John Davies. Frank was back in the thick of the town that was known as Tinopolis or Sospan (Welsh for saucepan), one of its major items of production. It seems that metal was still in the blood.

Frank is on the back row, far right as you look at the photograph.

Llanelli in 1912 was a large, thriving and bustling manufacturing town. It was a centre of tinplate production. Tinplate is made by thinly coating sheets of wrought iron or steel with tin to prevent rusting. The docks were at the heart of the town bringing in raw materials for the rolling mills and factories and taking away the finished products and coal mined locally. At this time, new markets were opening up for tinplate products as the petroleum and canned food industries expanded. There were very many companies operating in the steel and tinplate industry in Llanelli. One of the biggest was Llanelli Steelworks known locally known as the Klondike. For decades, the works dominated the landscape, its huge chimneys belching out smoke that often engulfed the whole town. The pay was good but the working conditions far less so. Men and boys worked alongside each other in a hot, oppressive atmosphere where injury and death were commonplace.

A visitor to any major town in the early 1900s would have witnessed the slow and at times uncomfortable move from horse-drawn transport to that powered by the combustion engine. Llanelli was no exception. When a fire broke out only a few years before, one of the biggest factors determining the speed of response had been how quickly the horses could be harnessed up to the fire tender. But by 1912, Llanelli had embraced the motor car to such an extent that a Llanellyite had invented something that was to give rise to an international manufacturing industry: a local business making spare wheels for this new mode of transport.

I spent some time as a child in Llanelli in the 1950s. The things I recall of it at that time were that it was a busy town with a prodigious number of public houses. On Station Road it seemed as though every other building was a hostelry and you could smell beer from the Rolling Mill at the corner of Lakefield Road with Station Road nearly up to the Town Hall! From my research for this chapter, I think that there were many aspects of Llanelli in the 1950s that were little different from the town in the early part of the 20th century.

My father loved to relate tales that his father had told him about the Llanelli hostelries in the 1910s. Down by the docks was a public house kept by a man called Hookey Hughes, so called because he was always on the lookout for ways to hook people into a scam to make a bob or two. One Christmas time, Hookey decided to run a raffle with the usual prizes of poultry and meat. When the tickets had been sold, a regular customer asked who had won what. Hookey replied, *'The wife's father had won first prize. Wasn't that lucky?'* As he related the list of prize winners, it turned out that his family was exceedingly lucky. His wife's brother had won and even he, Hookey, had won. At the finish, Hookey reminded the customer that he had not yet paid for his tickets to which came the reply, *'Wasn't I bloody lucky too!'*

In a pub called North Gate, an American sailor had bought some wonderful medicine that it was claimed prevented malaria and all the symptoms of the disease. The stuff was called quinine bitters and was made locally. The label on the product showed a huge warehouse and factory which was supposed to be the place where it was made and a picture of ships and the docks presumably to illustrate the import and export associated with this fine product. So impressed was he by the magnificent buildings on the label that the sailor asked if someone would show him them. In fact the medicine was made in scruffy premises in a nearby back alley. When the sailor was shown the back street he felt he was being made fool of and a fight broke out. The police were called and in the melee and struggle to restore order, several arrests were made with fines applied the following day for brawling and disturbing the peace. When the dust had settled and the sailor was convinced that the back alley really was where the medicine was made, he exclaimed that the advertisers were a lying lot of buggers! All ended well when the sailor paid for the other men's fines and bought them drinks.

In the Cambrian Inn in Seaside, the landlord was very ill, so ill in fact that the doctor had told the man's wife that he would not live much longer. His wife, not wishing to be caught unprepared, told the local undertaker who said he would come round and see his next client. The landlord by this time was in some kind of coma and the undertaker at the wife's request was sitting by his bed. As this point, to everyone's surprise, the patient came to. On seeing the undertaker, he said, *'Good God can't you wait for me to die? Must you come and size things up now?'* before slumping back into unconsciousness. The shock of all this seemed to work wonders for the following day the publican fully regained consciousness. Not only did he recover, he outlived the undertaker, the doctor and his wife and married again!

If the town of Llanelli was well supplied with drinking houses, it was equally well supplied with a developing network of houses of God in the form of churches and chapels. Within its boundaries it boasted: Church of England (later becoming Church in Wales), Baptists (Welsh) Baptists (English), Independent (Welsh), Independent (English), Calvinistic Methodist (Welsh), Calvinistic (English), Congregational, Presbyterian, Salvation Army, a Jewish Synagogue and a Roman Catholic Church. Chapels had splendidly Old Testament names: Carmel; Moriah; and Horeb to name but a few. Many had had been revitalised in the recent decade during the great Welsh religious revivals of 1904 and 1905.

In 1912, the town received a gift that year from Sir Stafford and Lady Howard. The gift was a park that Sir Stafford had bought the previous year with the intention of bequeathing it to the town to celebrate his earlier marriage. The park was given at an annual rent of five shillings for 999 years on condition that it would be ready within eight months so that it could be opened by the time of the couple's first wedding anniversary. It was finished in time, but only because of a coalminers' strike during 1912. Thousands of men who had been put out of work by the strike eagerly took on the work of building the park. The park opened in September 1912 to the jubilation of enormous crowds who gathered to cheer their appreciation of Sir Stafford and Lady Howard. As a result of the Howard family generosity, Llanelli could boast it had one of the best open spaces in the whole of South Wales.

In May that year, most of the residents of Llanelli had their first sight of an aeroplane. In an exciting venture sponsored by the Daily Mail, an aircraft landed in Llanelli: a Bleriot monoplane piloted by a Frenchman Monsieur Salmet. The police, including Frank, were there en masse to control the crowds that had gathered as word spread of what was about to happen. The plane landed in the outfields of Stradey. A cricket match taking place was hastily abandoned. Revealing something of the scope of people's vision at the time, the locals were amazed by the fact that the aeroplane had only taken ten minutes to fly from Swansea to Llanelli. To the delight of the assembled hordes there late in the afternoon, the pilot performed a display of aeronautics locally and around Swansea Bay and Mumbles before landing once again in Llanelli. The pilot took off for Somerset later in the week to the cheers of a further eager throng of thousands. Monsieur Salmet's visit became the talk of the town and the tale lived on as it was extensively reported through the local press and in a news film in the Picturedrome.

While the town of Llanelli was prosperous and revealing signs of that prosperity in its municipal growth, the living conditions revealed in the census returns of the time show a town of great contrasts.

In Queen Victoria Road, there was quiet respectability and enough wealth to afford up to four servants in some households such as those of the two surgeons who lived next door to one another in 1911. Even middle class merchants and manufacturers' families like that of the hemp rope manufacturer from Scotland could afford a servant, as could the family of a Baptist minister.

I was interested to note John Bowen Williams, described as Her Majesty's Sub Inspector of Schools, and his bank clerk son were languishing here in an eleven-roomed house with two servants. I can only conclude that Mr Williams had some private means because he would have been on a low salary and would have had little prospect of advancement being generally seen as a 'bag carrier' for other inspectors.

Several elderly people and a couple of widows lived on their own means in Queen Victoria Road each with a servant. The main occupants living spaciously in this road of smart houses were people from Llanelli and neighbouring villages, but alongside were also individuals from many different parts of the world: a pawnbroker from Germany; a glass merchant from Russia; a master draper from Reading; a couple with children who had been born in South Africa, perhaps when their parents went out there during the gold or diamond rush. The Jewish Synagogue was built there in 1909, thus providing the local Jewish population a permanent place of worship that they had hitherto had to go to Swansea to find.

But just streets away in Seaside, on the other side of the railway track, many families lived in overcrowded homes with few facilities. In this part of town, it was not unusual to find a large family of mother, father, and several children living in two or three rooms.

Frank and his family lived at 37 Andrew Street when they first moved to Llanelli, the house where PC John Davies and his family had lived before he moved out to Pwll. The two policemen had not only swapped jobs but houses too. These surprisingly large (six rooms) pebble-dashed terraced houses are still there today and are typical of many in the town. Take away the cars and satellite dishes and they would look as they looked a hundred years ago. The street was full of industrious people, such as: baker; fitter, brewer's clerk; grocers; teacher; joiner; and a lone commercial traveller with a servant as a live-in housekeeper. Some of those who lived alone, or with few other family members, let out rooms to lodgers to provide their sole means of support or an additional income. Those with as many as ten children also lived in their six rooms. But this was a time when bedrooms were for sleeping in and not having a bedroom of your own was not regarded as a measure of poverty.

People may have moved into large towns but their rural roots were not easily lost. The Lewis family kept hens in the garden. My father's sister, Isabel, recalled in the 1990s from 80 years past, her 2 year old sister Vi running down the path towards the house with eggs dropping out of her pinafore as she ran excitedly to show off her discovery.

As a police constable (now 1st class), Frank's wages would have been under £2 a week. The local newspaper ran a story about police pay in July 1914. In a place like Llanelli, where the expense of living was comparatively high, a serving constable received £1.13s.1d per week and that after 15 years' service.

Frank's uniform was made of worsted wool and the only protective gear he had was his helmet, a large cape and a truncheon. The cape became very heavy when it was wet and he might call in at home to try and dry out a little on very wet days.

My father reckoned that Frank never progressed any further than being a constable because he refused to join the Freemasons, seemingly a prerequisite at that time.

While he was in Llanelli, Frank became a mounted policeman for special occasions where there were large crowds such as carnivals. Because of his service with the Royal Horse Artillery, he was a natural to be chosen to ride a horse on duty. He was very proud of his horse and took his children to see the animals that he loved so much in the stables in Sunninghill Terrace. Frank used blanco, a whitener he would have used in the army, on the horse's lower legs to make it look its best for parade.

The constabulary was reviewed every three months or so by inspectors sent from headquarters. The inspectors asked each of the men in turn if they took a drink. It seems that all except Frank said that they did not. Included in the parade were those noted for their ability to quaff a few pints. One such officer called Kennedy was known to be catered for with pints of beer whilst he was on duty. When the parade was over, the inspector came over to Frank and said, *'I am certain that you were the only one on parade this morning to tell the truth.'*

This photograph shows Frank proudly seated in full uniform on his horse (Dick). A framed version of this photograph was on the wall of one of the bedrooms in the house in which I grew up.

War, again!

Fate seems to determine the degree to which the two world wars directly affected people in a family. You read heartrending tales of whole families of fathers, sons and brothers being wiped out in the carnage that was the Great War; the blighted families of men killed in action or maimed forever and whole generations of possible descendants lost forever. Yet in our family there were no terrible tales of such things and this left me wondering why. My conclusion was that it was largely a matter of the ages of the males in the family at the time that the war broke out.

Of nearly 130 officers in the Carmarthenshire Constabulary, 54 joined the armed services and 8 died in service in the Great War. In 1914, Frank Lewis at 45 was too old to be called up for active service. Within a year he would no longer be in the police force.

Frank's sons, aged 11 and 9, mercifully, were too young to be in the army. But some of the sons of Frank's sisters were of an age to be recruited to the war effort. His oldest sister, Mary (Polly) Foster had two sons who joined the army at the outbreak of the war: Charles Foster joined the Durham Light Infantry and his younger brother – another William Francis also joined the army. John (Jack) Alfred Benson, the son of his sister Rachel, was 21 and still living with Frank and family when they moved to Llanelli. He was called up not long after the war broke out.

Just before Christmas in 1914, Frank's thoughts might well have strayed back to the North East of England. In the news it was reported that German battle cruisers had loomed out of the mist in Hartlepool and for nearly an hour the town was bombarded with over a thousand shells. One hundred and two people were killed and some 400 were wounded. There was major damage to buildings and the shockwaves to morale were immense. Although the war on the continent had been waging for months, it had been centuries since any hostile attack had taken place on British soil. The attack on Hartlepool was part of a wider affront that also saw Scarborough and Whitby shelled.

The action of the German battle cruisers was the signal for many men in the area and beyond to join up via army and navy recruitment offices. Enlisting posters were drawn up showing a helmeted Brittannia, flag in one hand and sword in the other with the title 'Remember Scarborough' and the slogan, 'Enlist now'. Although the casualties were higher in Hartlepool, the authorities may have chosen Scarborough for the poster because of its wider popularity as a seaside holiday resort.

In the family, Harold Sengelow from Hartlepool was already in the navy and he served in the Great War. Harold's younger brother Frederick (5'5" tall and just 7 stones in weight) joined the East Sussex Regiment as a motorcycle rider.

Llanelli responded as did other cities, towns and villages up and down the land. There was scarcely a street in the town which did not send someone to war either as a reservist or a territorial. Men were eager to go to do their duty as Frank had been 15 years ago at the start of the war in South Africa. Horses were bought up on behalf of the Government. People gathered singing patriotic songs. The Llanelli Rugby Club met and passed a resolution that they would cancel all fixtures during such time as the war lasted. I can't help but think that there would not have been any players even had they agreed to continue with their fixtures, but the gesture was a decent one. Within Llanelli, there was a growing unease about the Germans in the town. In October 1914, employees of the Llanelly Tinstamping Works came out on strike as a protest against the employment of foreign workers, one a German and the other an Austrian. Even though the German had been employed in the works for the previous 14 years, the strikers had their way and the men in question were sacked from the works within days of the strike.

In 1915, wives and children of soldiers at the front marched in a recruitment rally in the town. Carrying a banner with the inscription, *'Our menfolk are at the front; where are yours???'*, the procession followed the Town Band along with territorials, boy scouts and the Red Cross Ambulance Brigade. Men who looked to be old enough to be in the army had a hard time explaining why they were not at the front.

The following year, the police and army officials carried out a raid at a race meeting rounding up about 30 men who could not give satisfactory accounts as to why they were not 'in khaki'. One means of avoiding service was for those passed fit to serve to later join a munitions factory. Men caught evading service were fined £2 and handed over to the military.

As time wore on, news of casualties and honours gained in battle seeped back to the town. A 23 year old man, Sergeant Ivor Rees, became the first man to be awarded the Victoria Cross (VC), *'for most conspicuous bravery in attack'*. He was awarded £100 by a local steelworks. Messrs Richard Thomas and Co. Coincidentally, Ivor Rees had worked for Messrs Richard Thomas and Co before being called up. The firm had promised the sum, worth about £4,000 today, to the first VC awarded to a Llanelli man. I only hope he made it home to realise his award.

By the beginning of 1918, the true cost of the war was all too clear. The local newspaper appealed for funds for the town's soldiers and sailors held captive in Germany. The funds were spent on parcels that were sent out, three each month, at a cost of £32 per year per man.

As if the war was not enough, the Spanish influenza outbreak was becoming a pandemic and had laid low hundreds and killed a score within a month of its appearance in Llanelli. Frank would have known only too well the danger of influenza as it was that which had just made a widow of his elder sister Rachel up in the North East. By 1920, the influenza pandemic claimed the lives worldwide of between 50 and 100 million. Although the war was not directly responsible for the influenza pandemic, the large movement of troops who had lived at close quarters, plus the fact that very many of the men were malnourished and therefore had weakened immune systems certainly hastened the virus' effect. Tragically, many men who had survived the atrocities of the trenches in the Great War were killed by this strain of the H1N1 virus that we know nowadays as avian or bird 'flu.

Because Frank's children were so young, their memories of the Great War were childlike. Isabel remembered having just recovered from scarlet fever before the war was declared. Her brothers had been kept home from school because of the risk of infection and were driving their mother mad. She also remembered going to the railway station with her mother to see Cousin Jack off on what might have been his last adventure. He was first billeted in Neyland in Pembrokeshire. The family kept in touch with him and Isabel (aged 5) and her mother went to see him in Neyland. Rather than the terrible war to which her cousin was bound, Isabel's memory of the day was of eating thick pieces of home-made bread and jam and being given a gift from her mother on the way home of a bowl with the letters of the alphabet around it.

In Llanelli itself during the war, life continued for the younger children much as before. The children each had their jobs to do at home before going to school. One week Denton cleaned all the boots and shoes, the next week Kenneth would do this chore. The fire had to be lit and the oven black-leaded every day. The cutlery had to be cleaned with metal polish every week. Being older than the girls, the boys got their own breakfast and then went off to school. If they were late, all the classroom doors were closed and they lined up in fear with the other latecomers. After a suitable psychological wait, out came the headmaster. If he was in a bad mood, he would cane the boys.

Whilst they were of primary school age, the children attended Lakefield School. Later in life, Isabel and her husband worked at this school as the cleaner and caretaker. I, too, attended the school for a few months when I lived with Isabel and Eric as a nine year old. I also visited the school over 30 years later as a school inspector.

When she was in her 80s, Isabel recalled an incident as a child at school in the yard when an airship had passed low overhead. The children were so excited that they ran, en masse, out of the yard trying to keep sight of this strange airborne object. Thinking only of what was in front of them, the children ended up on the beach about half a mile away. On returning to school they found themselves in trouble, but the enjoyment of the adventure was the more lasting memory.

On 11 November 1918, Isabel, then aged 9, heard the bells of the Parish Church ringing to mark the signing of the Armistice. She was allowed to go with a Catholic friend to the Roman Catholic Church to celebrate. The factories joined in the signalling of the end of the war by sounding hooters. The streets of Llanelli were thronged with cheering crowds as men and women in factories downed tools and rushed up to the town. Flags were hoisted and the Government suspended, for a week, the lighting and heating order that had been imposed allowing cafes and theatres to function as usual. Street lighting was restored and firework displays could be held to celebrate. Soldiers celebrated peace by marching around the town with those disabled by the war following on in five conveyances. As in every place in the land, there were many hundreds in the town whose husbands, fathers, sons and brothers would not return.

Miraculously, all of the men in the wider family, the Fosters, the Bensons, and the Sengelows, came back from the war, but not unscathed. Charles Foster was badly wounded and was permanently disabled because of a leg injury. He spent a lot of time in Dunstan Hill Hospital in Gateshead which in 1914 was converted into an orthopaedic hospital. Such were Charles' experiences at the front that he said if ever Germany took over Great Britain he would shoot all of his family and then shoot himself. Frederick Sengelow had a gunshot wound to his left arm and was awarded a payment of £35 for the damage it had caused. I hope he invested the money wisely as within two years of the end of the war, money was worth half the value it would have had a few years earlier.

Civvy Street, but not for long...

In the midst of the war, on 7th March 1915, Frank resigned from the police force, '...*being incapacitated for the performance of his duty by bodily infirmity (deafness)*'. Those years in the Boer War standing next to exploding 12 pounder guns had taken their toll.

Frank retired after 17 years 225 days with the Carmarthenshire Constabulary on a pension of £29.9s.5d per year. This pension sum would have had the same spending power as £1,269 in 2005. Clearly police constables nowadays are paid a lot more actually and proportionately; I calculate that a similarly experienced constable retiring now after 17 years' service would have a pension of over £7,000.

Frank's career with the police force had been exemplary. The only item listed under 'Misconduct' being, '...*was ordered for Active Service to South Africa on 21st Oct 1899*'. I can only think that there was nowhere else on the officer's record sheet to record such a thing as it can hardly be said to have been misconduct to obey an order to re-join the army whilst a reservist.

The family had to move house yet again following Frank's retirement, presumably to allow the next police constable to take up residence in Andrew Street. Frank also had to find new work as the pension was not enough to keep his family of five. He did what many ex-policemen have done over the years; he decided to invest some of his money in taking on the tenancy of a public house. The Bryn Terrace Hotel, Llanelli became the next family home.

The Bryn Terrace Hotel sounds quite grand but it was in fact one of many public houses in the docks area of Llanelli. It was not a hotel in the sense we would use the word today, more just a drinking house. The painted sign on the gable end of the place was still just about visible in the 1980s long after it had ceased to be a public house. When Frank was the landlord, the hotel was also the meeting place of the Llanelli Branch of the Merthyr Unity Philanthropic Society. There were scores of so-called friendly societies all over Wales. They each made one of the local pubs their meeting place. Before the creation of a welfare state, friendly societies provided financial and social services to individuals in the form of a kind of insurance policy. The societies often had religious, political, or trade affiliations. Frank himself was a member of one of the oldest such friendly societies, Hearts of Oak, whose origins lay in London in 1842. No doubt having seen his father have to go into the workhouse when he became too ill to work was an incentive to Frank to make some sort of cover arrangements for himself and his family. I was quite pleased to learn that Hearts of Oak was one of the first friendly societies to admit women.

The photograph below shows Frank at the rear of the picture, nearest to the door of the Bryn Terrace Hotel. My father (then aged about 10) is standing in front of him, the two of them dressed rather snazzily in matching plus fours and straw boaters. They are pictured about to set off for a day trip to the seaside, Porthcawl I think, in the large cars pictured with them. With the exception of the other boy, who was presumably company for Kenneth, all of the others appear to be older men. Taken in 1915 or 1916, all of the younger men in the place would presumably have been away at war. The fact that Denton, my father's elder brother, was not in the picture may imply that, aged 13, he was at work.

Having grown up in a pub, Mary Lewis would no doubt have helped in running the Bryn Terrace Hotel. Frank, as an ex-policeman and a tall and strong man, would have been on hand to deal with any awkward customers. And there were some such characters in this dockside part of Llanelli as his work in the police force had taught him.

In the Llanelly and County Guardian it was reported that on 16 December 1915 one Thomas Davies of Catherine Street was charged with drunkenness and refusing to quit the Bryn Terrace Hotel on 4 December. Frank Lewis, the landlord, gave evidence of the incident in the Magistrates' Court and the man was fined.

While the family lived in Bryn Terrace, Kenneth and his friends crossed a bridge over the Great Western Railway line each day on their way to school, a bridge known locally as Devil's Bridge. On one fine summer's day leading up to the school holidays, something of the devil must have got into the boys. Spotting a number of railway vans being shunted into a side line, they decided, on a whim, to explore the said vans to see what was in them.

By now they were playing truant or 'mitching' as it is known in South Wales. The boys crawled through the fence at the rail side and hid from view under the bridge until all was clear. To their delight, when they went into the vans they found some cases of oranges and bananas that had not been unloaded. Off they went back under the bridge, lit a fire (nothing, it seems, was real unless you had a fire going) and shared out the spoils. The one drawback of their haul was that the bananas were on the green side as they had been brought in from the West Indies and were being allowed to ripen before being sold; the oranges on the other hand were rather ripe. By the end of the day, the four boys were not in very good shape. To make matters worse, they had to stay in their lair until late afternoon, as they could not risk going home before school finished.

That night the father of one of the other boys came into the pub and asked Frank how Kenneth was feeling as his own son, John Mathias, was sick and had diarrhoea. Kenneth was alright. But, feeling sorry for himself, John had told his father the story of the boys' day. That night was an uncomfortable one for Kenneth. Frank took his responsibilities as an ex-policeman very seriously. Not only did Kenneth get a good hiding, but he was put on bread and water for 24 hours and lost his pocket money for two weeks. The only consolation for him was that Frank wrote him a note to take to school saying he was not to be punished any more by the head of the school as he had already received enough at home.

Frank's life as a publican did not last very long. Perhaps being in the midst of the Great War was not the best time to make money in a public house when many of his possible customers were away serving King and country. Perhaps, too, it was not a good idea to have Mary so close to available drink. After about 15 months, Frank was back in uniform. This time he was a commissionaire or security officer at the local Glanmor Foundry.

The Foundry had its beginnings in 1850 when Frank's father had been making his way out of West Wales for Merthyr Tydfil. The works covered several acres and at its height employed over 400 men. Families of men and boys worked there with skills being passed on from one generation to the next. The firm specialised in moulding and casting for the tinplate industry and played an important role in Llanelli's prosperity.

Frank was really a policeman again in a very smart uniform policing the foundry to make sure that everything was in order.

Leaving the pub meant moving house again. This time the Lewis family moved to Landas House, Caersalem Terrace in Llanelli. This place was near to the railway station: a large terraced house with seven rooms.

Typically these houses had a front door which led into a passage off which were: a front room that was rarely used; a middle room, again not regularly used; and at the end of the passage, a living room. The living room would have had a black range with oven to one side and a hob for the kettle to sit over the fire. Food would be eaten in the living room and there would be an armchair or two. Nobody locked their front doors, even as late as the 1960s when I used to visit my aunt and uncle in a similar house in Llanelli. One day when Isabel was quite young, she was coming out of the kitchen to go along the passage and upstairs to bed when a man came staggering out of their middle room. He must have looked a ridiculous sight as he was wearing Isabel's hat that sported a bunch of cherries. Her father, alerted by Isabel's shriek, jumped up from the armchair in the living room and told the man to get out. The drunk became abusive and refused to go. With that, Frank sent the man a blow to the chin knocking him along the passage before helping him further on his way through the front door.

The side of their home in Caersalem Terrace faced a yard at the back of tobacconist and sweet shops in Station Road owned by a German Jewish family, Mr and Mrs Wyman. But this was not entirely urban living. The Wymans kept a cow in the back yard of the shop. They kept the cow to make cheese which was hung to dry in a bag on their clothes line in the garden. The Lewis children delighted in taking the cow on a lead to nearby common ground so that it could graze on better pasture.

In 1918, there were a number of notable family events. On Thursday 23 May, his 13th birthday, Kenneth went to school as usual. At the end of the morning, he left school for good. By 2.00pm Kenneth had started work where his father and brother were, at the Glanmor Foundry.

At first, he was a 'go-fer' for the men in the foundry and no doubt had his fair share of trying to find glass hammers and other impossible things until he became wise to the ploys of the older workers. He was a quick learner and stayed at the foundry for 10 years, learning his trade as a welder.

Aged 41, and perhaps as something of a surprise, Mary found herself pregnant again that year. One month after the Armistice, on 11 December 1918, the last of that generation of Lewis children (Primrose Vera Jennie) was born, the psychic seventh child of the seventh child of a seventh child.

Aged 9, her oldest sister Isabel had not known that there was a new baby expected: quite unlikely that this would be the case nowadays. The baby arrived during the night and the girls Isabel and Vi were woken up to see the new arrival. When they came into the room where their mother was with the baby, their two older brothers were already there dressed in their nightshirts. Over 70 years later, Isabel remembered being so excited that she could not sleep for the rest of the night. She wanted to be the first to run round to tell the neighbours; as she said, '...*as if they did not know already!*'

The Roaring Twenties:
two weddings and a funeral

The 1920s ushered in an era of excitement on a range of fronts. The Great War formed the backcloth to the decade. There were those who had been cruelly bereaved. There were women who would never marry as the men they had loved had been killed in the war. And there were those who had been permanently damaged in body and mind by what they had experienced at the front. Men and some women had seen things their older and younger friends and family could not have imagined. Life had changed on a scale and in ways that surely would never be repeated.

Many returning from war were keen to have fun and to try and forget the horrors and deprivations they had experienced. Life was to be lived as so many had lost theirs.

Inventions like the wireless and gramophones brought music into people's homes, including the new jazz. Cinemas grew up in towns and cities around the land. For a few pence a week, the movies brought stars of the silent films direct to the masses. Stars such as Harold Lloyd, Charlie Chaplin, Greta Garbo and Buster Keaton became favourites. Dancing in halls became a popular pastime and sports such as tennis and cycling took hold.

The growth of public libraries allowed ordinary working people access to books for self-improvement and escapism. Thrillers and mysteries were particularly popular, especially the novels of Agatha Christie and Edgar Wallace.

In the Lewis household, the 1920s started with great excitement. Mary had entered a photograph of her 11 year old daughter, Isabel, in a children's beauty competition run by the Daily Mirror. To everyone's delight, Isabel was chosen as one of the 'probables'.

She was invited to attend for the judging at the Savoy Hotel in London. The Savoy: the last word in elegance and opulence! This must have been quite an experience. The Savoy had opened in 1889, built by the impresario Richard D'Oyly Carte whose famous opera company brought the popular Gilbert and Sullivan operas to the theatre. It was a magnificent Edwardian place in the Strand with spectacular views of the Thames, the first luxury hotel to introduce electric lighting.

Isabel aged 11

Isabel's proud parents went with her for her big day. She was not the winner, but 80 years on, Isabel still remembered the lovely time they had enjoyed and the excitement of visiting London as such a young girl.

The following year, when she was 12 years old, Isabel became the first in her family to carry on with her schooling to a higher grade in a new school in Llanelli: Stebonheath Central. There was a two mile walk to and from school each day. There were no school buses in those days and there was no tram route anywhere near. It was too far for Isabel to walk home for lunch so her mother gave her a packet of sandwiches. On fine days, she ate her lunch on the waste land opposite the school along with a drink of raspberry flavoured pop which she came to dislike.

Instead of the basic three Rs, the curriculum opened out into exotic subjects like French, botany (zoology was too risqué!), and algebra. The pupils sat on chairs at tables instead of using heavy Victorian desks with attached tip up seats. After a few months, the corridor was stacked with broken chairs. The novelty of the pupils being able to balance the chairs backwards on two legs had taken its toll on the furniture. A laboratory was added to the building at a later date. In the adjoining school yard,

Isabel aged 12

there was a cottage with a dining kitchen and bedroom. In the cottage, the girls were given housewifery lessons during which they were taught how to cook and clean.

The new school emulated the local private school by having a uniform. In what seems like a very modern thing to do, the children helped to choose their uniform. They even modelled the school hat for the girls on Isabel's head, choosing a Dutch style cap with a peak each side and a badge on the front.

But, sadly, Isabel's formal education was to come to an end before long. In 1923, Isabel, aged 14, left school to help her mother at home. Mary Lewis was unwell and there were two younger girls to be cared for. The younger sisters' education never progressed beyond the elementary school.

After Isabel had left school, her weekly treat was to go to a dancing class held in a local school room. One time there was to be a flannel dance where all the males had to wear white flannel cricket trousers and white shirts. She could barely contain her excitement as the big night approached. Imagine her dismay when her father insisted she had to be at home by 10.00pm, even though the event was to go on until midnight. After bawling her eyes out, her mother agreed to accompany her so that she could stay until the end. Fancy a teenager today being accompanied by her mother to the school prom! As things turned out, that night out was to be one of the last occasions that Isabel's mother went anywhere.

The week before his 20th birthday in May 1925, Kenneth went to his mother's room to take her a cup of tea before he went to work. His mother asked him to draw the curtains, took the tea from him and said, *'You're a good boy, Kenneth.'* Later that day, Mary Valentine died with Frank by her side.

My father always attributed his mother's death to a liking for the bottle gained during the years that she had lived in a public house. The certificated causes of death were cardiac syncope (basically her heart stopped without warning), acute gastritis and chronic bronchitis. She was only 48 but to my mind the next picture shows she looked much older.

This is last photograph taken of Mary Valentine Lewis in the 1920s. She could only have been in her forties but looks much older.

Things in the Lewis household changed considerably, and not all for the better.

There was still a young child, the 7 year old Vera, to be looked after. Her older sisters Isabel (16) and Vi (14) saw to that initially. Frank's wider family also rallied, led by his elder sister Mary (Polly) Foster. She came all the way from Tyneside to look after the family for a short while, bringing with her Alice, her daughter, and Frankie Foster, her grandson.

After Polly returned home, Frank employed a housekeeper called Mrs Tracy. She did not last very long, as she drank heavily. The girls found empty gin bottles under her bed and she ran off with all their silver. The next housekeeper did not last very long either, crime unknown.

Things were unsettled. Frank was grieving for his wife and the house in Caersalem terrace was a constant reminder of her, especially the front room where she had lain before the funeral. But life continued there a while.

As soon as Mary died, the door to the front room where she lay had a small brass bolt fitted on the outside to remind people not to go in. The body was washed and prepared in that room in readiness for people to come in and pay their respects before the funeral. A local woman was paid to do the so-called 'laying out'. Months after the funeral, the bolt on the door caused a family argument. Isabel absent-mindedly shot the bolt closed as she walked along the passage. Sometime later she was aware of shouting and banging from the front room. When she opened the door, her furious elder brother Denton flew out angrily telling her that he had been in the room choosing a horse on which to place a bet. By the time he had been let out of the room, the race had run. At the tea table, things were rather tense but thankfully the horse had not romped home in one of the first three places so Isabel's bacon was saved.

Later in the year that his mother had died, Denton gave up his job as a crane driver in the Glanmor Foundry to follow in his father's footsteps by becoming a policeman. Within a few months he was stationed in Ammanford and was no longer living at home.

In May 1926, the whole of the UK was embroiled in a General Strike. The strike was called by the Trades Union Congress to try and prevent the Government's worsening of the coal miners' pay and conditions. Although the strike did not last long, nine days in fact, it had a profound effect on the country. It also coloured Kenneth's views on striking for the rest of his life.

In 1927, Frank moved with his younger son, Kenneth, and his three daughters, Isabel, Vi and Vera, to a brand new home in Gower View, Llanelli. As the name suggests, these properties were high up in the town, looking out over Carmarthen Bay and across to Gower. He had literally moved up in the world, out of the terraced houses of the town to where you could breathe and enjoy the view.

There was a lot to be done. Frank engaged another housekeeper and enlisted the help of some of the men from the Glanmor Foundry to help him with digging the garden. One day, a man called Eric James was one of the men who came to dig the garden. Eric's father and Frank had been in the police force at the same time. In fact, William James, Eric's father, is in the same group photograph shown earlier: as you look at the photograph, he is in front of and to the left of the man in the bowler hat.

While the digging was done, Frank was indoors preparing a meal for the men to eat. Ever after, Eric remembered the day's digging because of the dinner that Frank had prepared, a huge plate of 15 lamb chops, more than he had ever seen! Isabel had already met Eric at a bus stop one night when she was coming home from Burry Port where she had visited her friend. He had gallantly helped her on and off the bus and asked if he could walk her home. It was love at first sight.

Love must have been in the clean air in Gower View. Kenneth was also courting, but his sisters were very unhappy at his choice of the bride-to-be: Elizabeth Janet Annie Gray who worked at a cinema in Llanelli. Kenneth paid no heed, but later wished he had. On 4 December 1927, aged 22, Kenneth became the first of the brothers and sisters to get married. The wedding took place in the parish church in the centre of Llanelli. He and his wife moved into a neat little semi-detached bungalow in New Zealand Street, Llanelli, not far from the rugby and cricket grounds.

In the summer of 1928, Carmarthenshire became known around the world as news got out that the first woman to fly across the Atlantic had landed in Carmarthen Bay near to Pwll in the seaplane, 'Friendship'. The flight had taken 20 hours and 40 minutes. Amelia Earhart and her crew of two, Wilmer Stultz and Louis Gordon, mistakenly believed they had landed in Ireland. From their plane they were brought by boat into nearby Burry Port harbour. Their landing became a focus for hundreds of people who flocked to Burry Port from Swansea, Cardiff and London. Crowds hung around the small coastal village for days hoping for a glimpse of the plane and its occupants. Not to miss out, Kenneth and a friend went down to Burry Port and saw Miss Earhart and her crew set off back to the USA via Southampton. They were close enough to her to hear her speak in her American (Kansas) drawl, something they had not heard before.

Later that year, Denton married Lilian Thomas in Abergwili Church. Denton had met his bride-to-be in Ammanford. Isabel was the only bridesmaid, a curious snub to his other two sisters. I met Auntie Lilian in the late 1950s when she was on the same circuit of whist drives that Auntie Isabel and Uncle Eric used to attend. She did not seem much like an auntie compared with Isabel. She seemed rather aloof and to deem herself to be in a different class from the rest of the family. Whether this was real or affected, I do not know.

As the only bridesmaid, one of Isabel's duties was to join the best man in a car accompanying the bride and groom to Cardiff where the happy couple were to catch a train for their honeymoon destination. Denton had not liked this plan as he seemed not to trust his best man, one PC Crout, with his sister. Constable Crout had plans to take Isabel to the theatre in Cardiff. In the event, the car broke down. A replacement car had to be found to take Denton and his wife at speed to Cardiff and Isabel had to wait for another car to take her and the thwarted Crout back home.

Round about the time that Denton was getting married, Kenneth's world fell apart. He had to admit that his sisters' warnings were right and that he had made a bad mistake. Within a year, his wife had run off with the manager of the local cinema. He did the only thing he could think of. Like his grandfather had done some 80 years before, he left Wales. His departure led to a life in different parts of the UK. He would never go back to his wife and he would not go back to live in Wales for nearly 60 years. His adventures were just beginning.

Kenneth: setting the scene

While I was putting together this book, I had imagined that once I reached this section I would find the writing plain sailing. After all, I would be writing about my father whom I had known for well over forty years. The reality was to prove somewhat different. I actually felt a greater responsibility to get this part as right as possible because here was the first person in the lineage whom I had known personally rather than through artefacts and research. Here was someone whose personality was known to me at first hand and did not need to be reconstructed from supposition and speculation.

Nevertheless, I am struck by how little real detail about time and place I managed to glean from Kenneth whilst he was alive even though he would talk readily about his past and reminisce often about his exploits after leaving Wales. I suppose actual dates are not always that relevant in storytelling. If someone were to ask me whether from memory something happened in 1972 or 1973, I would have difficulty being exact unless that event was linked with something momentous in the year in question. So, as with the more distant forebears even some of Kenneth's story has had to be pieced together in a forensic way from snippets of information, known dates and documents.

Once again I am reminded of my hypothesis that people either move towards something or away from something. In Kenneth's case, it was definitely the latter. He moved away from Wales to escape what he felt was the personal humiliation at the hand of his wife of less than a year.

As children growing up, my brother and I had no idea that our father had been married before, nor for that matter that our mother, Elsie, had been widowed before she met our father. I discovered these bits of information one day in the mid-1960s when I came across my parents' marriage certificate as I was rooting around in a wardrobe. I don't know what I expected to see when I read the certificate, but I wasn't prepared for what I saw.

Not only had both our parents been married before, but they had not married each other until long after my brother and I were born. In fact the marriage had taken place just months before our mother had died. It may have been the 1960s that I discovered this when Britain was supposed to be swinging, but I can assure you that in small town Teesside, people were expected to be neatly married if they were living together, especially if they had children.

On the marriage certificate against Kenneth's name in the column headed 'Condition' was written, *'previous marriage dissolved'*. This phrase sounded quite mysterious, almost like some experiment in a laboratory where all traces of the previous state of matter could be transformed by simply adding water. My mother's description as a widow was a shock. I had always associated widowhood with old age, black clothes and sad faces.

I felt sure that my brother would know what all this meant, but he seemed as shocked as I was. After a long discussion, Tony, as the elder of the two of us, reluctantly agreed that he would ask Dad about it.

Once prompted, Kenneth sat down and, with the relief that comes from being able to tell something that has been kept secret, told us how he came to experience divorce, re-marriage and widower hood in less than twelve months. Some years on, Kenneth clearly still felt a range of deep emotions but the over-riding one seemed to be that we would not feel any less of him as a result of his not having told us before.

In short, he told us his first wife had left him not long after they were married. He left Wales not long after that and once he had done so he did not see or hear from his wife again until he learned in the late 1940s, via one of his sisters, that she had died. At last, in 1949, he was free to marry again and make an 'honest woman' of the mother of his children. And that might have been it. But the rumours of his first wife's demise were greatly exaggerated. Five years after he married Elsie, Kenneth was contacted by a solicitor. It seemed that his first wife was very much alive. She wanted to marry someone else and therefore wished to instigate divorce proceedings. Understandably, this was something of a stunner.

The only thing Kenneth could do was to go through with the divorce and then remarry Elsie. The timing was not the best as in 1954 Elsie had just discovered that she was terminally ill with cancer. Not surprisingly

Kenneth referred to those few years as the worst of his life. The divorce papers state that the marriage should be dissolved by reason that Kenneth's first wife had deserted him without cause for a period of at least three years preceding the presentation of the petition. The following month, Kenneth and Elsie were back at Stockton registry office for a second time. The legitimate marriage took place just months before Elsie died in 1955. The same two people, Thomas and Florence Dumain, were the witnesses to the marriage in 1949 and 1955. I had never heard of these people as friends of my Mam and Dad so I did a little research. I found that Thomas Dumain was a registrar in Stockton and Florence was his wife.

In the coming chapters I shall do my best to record some of Kenneth's tales, those things that seemed to be important to him and to have defined him in some way. I have drawn up a year-by-year list of known events in the time between 1927 when Kenneth had married his first wife, the wandering cinema attendant, and 1941 when my brother was born. I did the same for Elsie and cross matched the two. That time period proved to be an eventful one for both Elsie and Kenneth, separately and together.

A roaming decade

Choosing to move out of a safe job in late 1928 was perhaps not the most sensible of moves, but as Kenneth himself would say, he was not afraid of a challenge and he had only himself to think about by then.

Within a year of his leaving Wales, the Wall Street crash had taken place in America and the world economy plunged into what became known as the Great Depression. By the end of 1930, unemployment had more than doubled to 2.5 million – about 20% of the insured workforce.

Work was hard to come by, but Kenneth was never one to sit around waiting for a job to come to him. He had to work to live. He had no inherited wealth, or money from investments or the sale of a house. He had never owned any property, nor did he throughout the rest of his life. He was not one to saddle himself with personal belongings. During the 30s, he would have been able to pack all he had in a single suitcase. He could up sticks at fairly short notice and move to wherever there was work and lodgings to take him in for a reasonable rent.

The enormous railway infrastructure that existed in the UK at that time made it easy to move from one place to another in the way that motorways do today.

Once out of Wales, Kenneth lived in swift succession in Gloucester and London. He was not the first to think that the streets of London were paved with gold and not the first to find they were not. He stayed in London only a week. He could find no work and had to sleep rough on the Embankment. That time out of work made him determined not to repeat the experience.

Having tried his luck in the big smoke, he then moved northwards to Lancashire and Yorkshire. During the 1930s, he lived around Preston and Huddersfield, working in foundries where welders were in demand. The most important thing he took with him when he left Wales was a written testimonial from the Glanmor Foundry. He carried this piece of paper with him everywhere and kept it all his life, patching it up with tape on the reverse side so that it is still reasonably intact today. This piece of paper with its positive recommendations of Kenneth's trustworthiness and reliability was to help get him jobs where nobody knew him.

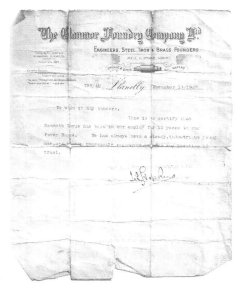

He lived in lodgings wherever he worked, places run by families or widowed women with a room to rent from which they could make some extra cash. One Mrs Murgatroyd was a landlady he recalled years later. Arriving home from work one evening, Kenneth was in more of a hurry than usual as he was going out with some of his mates to a local dance hall. After dining on tripe and onions, he went upstairs to wash and change into his best flannels and blazer. Imagine his surprise when he found that the wardrobe was empty. To his even bigger surprise, he found that the same Mrs Murgatroyd had pawned the clothes to get money to buy food for the meal he had just eaten. Leaving Mrs Murgatroyd in no doubt as to how he felt about the matter, Kenneth had to visit the pawnbroker to pay to have his own clothes back. Needless to say, Mrs M did not get her rent that week and Kenneth left the place as soon as possible.

While he was in Preston, Kenneth went on a weekend visit to Blackpool, an exciting place to be in the 1930s. Special trains and coaches brought thousands of visitors to the place to see the sights during the summer. The place was just as busy in the autumn when the famous illuminations were switched on: 200,000 lights fed by an electric supply from Preston's super power station. In the summer, the beaches were packed with day trippers and those able to take a week's holiday. In the afternoons and evenings, the action switched to the Tower Ballroom and the Winter Gardens. Tourists flocked to Blackpool Tower to hear Reginald Dixon the resident organist. Kenneth favoured the dancing in the Winter Gardens.

Just as well, because here he met a woman from Hull who was in her early 30s.

Elsie Stonehouse had been taken there by her friends following the sudden death of her husband of less than two years. The local newspaper was on the case with somewhat indecent haste. It reported, *'...while working at Messrs C E Rymer and Sons' mineral water factory in Cave Street, Hull this morning, Clarence Stonehouse (34), a married man, of Sharp*

Elsie

Street, collapsed and was seen to be bleeding from the mouth. A doctor was summoned, but Stonehouse died almost immediately. The Coroner has been informed.' Clarence had died from a tubercular haemorrhage.

The chance meeting of Kenneth and Elsie in the Winter Gardens was the start of a relationship that lasted nearly a quarter of a century, but it was not all plain sailing. Kenneth's wife may have left him, but he was still married and divorce was an expensive business for an ordinary working person. Also, Kenneth and Elsie may have met in Blackpool but neither of them lived there or even near to one another; so there began a long period of seeing one another when they could. Gradually Kenneth moved east across country and Elsie moved west from Hull. In Huddersfield, near Ravensknowle Park, they set up home together in a rented bungalow at 7 Felcote Avenue.

It was from here that one of Kenneth's biggest adventures took place.

The morning began like any other. Kenneth got up, rose early, had his breakfast, a bacon sandwich and a strong cup of tea. He did not know as he pulled on his overalls and slipped into his jacket that within an hour or so his life would have changed in a way he could not have imagined.

He kissed Elsie goodbye and made his way to work for another day of welding with his gang of labourers. Before he reached the works' gates, he met up with two of his mates and sensed straightaway that something was wrong. They explained their agitation. They had found out that other gangs of local welders and their mates were being paid 3 old pence (3d) an hour more than they were being paid. Not surprisingly this news did not go down well. Kenneth being the man he was went straight to the foreman. He said that he and his men were not happy at being short-changed and, in the spirit of Oliver Twist, he asked for more.

The foreman's response was summary: *'If you don't like it, you can bugger off!'*

Kenneth and gang did not like it and they decided to do as suggested and walked off the job. By mid-morning they had made their way to the local Labour Exchange to look for other jobs. What they had not bargained for was the continued meanness of the foreman who had rung up the Labour Exchange and had the men blacklisted. As they had walked away from jobs they already had, they could not be offered something else. However, the man in the Labour Exchange was slightly more compassionate and indicated that he could not stop them from looking at the notice board to see if there was anything suitable.

Combing through the postcards on the board they saw one that said, 'WELDERS WANTED - STOCKTON ON TEES'. Waiting only to figure out how to get there, Kenneth decided he had to go there as he could not face being out of work. He called back at home and let Elsie know what had happened and said he would send for her as soon as he had a job and somewhere to live. With that, he was off on a train for Stockton. By the time he arrived, it was 6.00pm and everywhere was shut for the day. With little money in his pocket, he stayed that night in the Salvation Army Hostel: one shilling a night for the bed and a mug of tea in the morning.

Next day, as soon as it was open, he was at the Labour Exchange looking for the whereabouts of the advertised job. He was shocked to find that although the welders were being recruited in Stockton, the job was actually nearly 300 miles north in Fort William in the highlands of Scotland. But, at least his rail fare was paid by the recruiting company. So, stopping only to send a telegram to Elsie, Kenneth headed for his new job in Scotland.

The work was on the hydroelectric power scheme in the area. He was responsible for welding the large water-carrying pipes that run down Ben Nevis. Men were employed here from all parts of the UK and Ireland. Kenneth worked for the English Electric Company and some of the Irish worked for a firm called Carmichael.

The men worked in all weathers: gales, torrential rain and snow being common all year round. Kenneth would often be soaked to the skin and in the days before specialist wet weather gear, a woollen coat was as good as it got. Kenneth picked up a phrase about the rainy weather which made him chuckle all his life. He was walking along a road one day in Fort William with the rain lashing down. He passed a farmer who bade him, *'Good morning'* and added as he passed, *'Kinda moist today.'*

Those with trades, like Kenneth, were housed in huts on the lower slopes of Ben Nevis. They were looked after by other men employed to keep the huts clean and to cook and wash clothes for the workers. Conditions in the navvies' huts owned by Carmichael were, by all accounts, somewhat different. Those huts were overcrowded and as one man came off a shift, he would kick out of a bunk a man whose turn it was to do the next shift. The men would sleep in their work clothes and even keep on their work boots. Cleaning in these huts comprised shaking out the blankets once a week. Food was cooked in a large cooking pot in the centre of the hut. Men would supplement their diet by using snares to catch rabbits to eat. After skinning and eviscerating their catches, the pieces of meat cooked in the pot along with unskinned potatoes and onions. The meat would be hung from string, attached to a particular anchor for later identification. After work, the men returned to identify their meat and eat it along with a share of the cooked vegetables. Fights would sometimes break out after an argument about whose meat was whose. Breakfast tea was left to brew overnight in the same greasy cooking pot after the 'stew' was eaten.

Life in and around the camps was simple and predictable with so many men living in close proximity. Gambling was rife. Arguments and fights would break out over the merest of slights or offences.

At noon on Saturday, the men queued up to receive their week's wages. Those with a change of clothes smartened themselves up. Those with only one set of clothes would make a nod in the direction of personal hygiene by washing the shirts from their backs in the local stream. After wringing out their shirts they would put them back on still wet. Having money in their pocket, most men were off to spend it. Off they went down the mountain and into the hostelries of Fort William. Several hours later, the byways and ditches that led back to the camps were littered with men sleeping off their purchases. Those who had got into fights were guaranteed time in the cells to come round and pay for their misdemeanours.

Elsie, meanwhile, had returned to live at her father's home in Sharp Street, Hull. Every three weeks, Kenneth had a weekend pass to take the train down to Hull to see her. This must have been a highlight in an otherwise miserable 5 years for Elsie. Between 1930 and 1935, Elsie suffered the death of her mother, one of her sisters, her first husband and her father.

Back in the Highlands, Kenneth's work brought him close to nature. He loved to see the rabbits, deer and upland birds and was in awe at seeing a golden eagle at very close quarters when it swooped down to warn him and his mates that their work was interfering with his eyrie. Although he loved to see animals, he was not sentimental about them and could catch a rabbit for food if he needed to. Kenneth had even tasted baked hedgehog whilst he was up there. He met a 'gentleman of the road' who showed him how to roll the animal in wet clay before cooking it in a wood fire. The hedgehog was cooked once the clay turned hard and black. The clay case was broken apart to reveal the meat which, you will not be surprised to read, tasted just like chicken!

One highlight for Kenneth and some of his mates was a visit to the local distillery. The men eagerly looked forward to receiving a free drink of whisky. After the tour they were taken to the manager's office. On the manager's desk was a small barrel. Asking about its contents, they were told that it contained whisky that was 100 degrees proof and far too strong for them to try. The men could not resist such a challenge and each was given a thimbleful of the tempting liquid. They derided the small quantity but found that when they were outside and the air hit them they were overpowered by it!

Kenneth spent another spell on a different hydroelectric power scheme in Scotland, that time in the lowland area of Dumfries and Galloway.

He expressed affection for his time in the Dalry and Castle Douglas area. But he had one tale that spoke volumes about the life and times in these transient developments. One evening at the time when gallons of concrete were being poured in to make the dam walls, Kenneth was putting away his gear in one of the sheds. A well-known bully of a foreman came in to the shed and looked around for a heavy shovel. Picking up a shovel, the foreman turned to Kenneth and told him that if he valued his life he would not have seen anything. During the following days, one of the labourers was reported missing. Kenneth's view was that the labourer had been killed by the foreman and then preserved in the concrete walls of the dam. Nobody came looking for the man and he was never seen again.

On Sundays at that time in Scotland, you could only get an alcoholic drink if you were a bona fide traveller, defined as someone who had journeyed at least three miles. Drinks could only be had in a hotel or inn rather than a public house as part of providing refreshments to weary travellers. One Sunday, Kenneth was in such a place enjoying a beverage when a policeman on a bike called in to check on the credentials of these 'travellers'. The constable did not entirely buy Kenneth's tale of having walked three miles, but kept up the pretence by offering to accompany Kenneth on his way home once he had finished his drink. Kenneth's illicit beverage was had at the expense of a three mile walk away from the town in which he lived. The policeman meanwhile rode his bike alongside. Once the policeman was out of sight, Kenneth's drink was then properly legitimised by his three mile walk back.

While he worked in Scotland, Kenneth was earning good money, much more than he had been used to. He always compared his work on the hydroelectric schemes with that taken on 40-50 years later by men on the North Sea oil rigs. The unsocial work in each case was able to attract a premium for those bold enough to take it.

Leader of the gang and part of the union

When the jobs were finished in Scotland, Kenneth returned to work in the North of England. He worked in various places that he knew, including Preston and Huddersfield. The photographs below with Kenneth in the centre in each were taken around that time. They show Kenneth very much as the leader of his welding gangs.

Kenneth in his trademark beret seated at the centre.

In 1936, he joined the Union of Boiler Makers and Iron Ship Builders which later became part of the General and Municipal Workers' Union (GMB). He joined in Bolton which it seems was the oldest continuous branch.

The union dated back to 1834 when it was set up as a friendly society for boiler makers. The objectives of the Friendly Boiler Makers Society

were stated to provide mutual relief in cases of sickness, old age, infirmity and for the burial of the dead.

Kenneth: kneeling centre about 1936.

The history of the union is well documented. The membership had to obey certain rituals and routines at meetings that seem, on reading, to be like being admitted to some form of freemasonry. I cannot imagine that my father was greatly enamoured of such things. I would imagine he became a member when he did to ensure work at a time of uncertainty, especially when he was not originally from the area. He would never strike and felt that the threat of industrial action was always more of a deterrent than striking itself. His experience had showed him that nothing was fully resolved unless everyone concerned had an opportunity to state their views and reach a shared agreement.

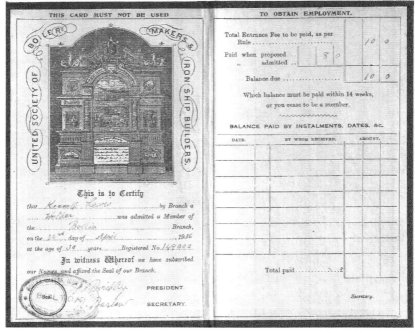

Kenneth's union card.

In 1986, and long after he had retired, Kenneth still received a Christmas message from the Secretary of the local branch to which he had belonged addressing him as 'Worthy Brother, dear Friend', and signed 'Yours fraternally', wishing him the compliments of the season. J W Turnbull of the Billingham Branch of the GMB and Allied Trades

Union had tracked him down to his new home in Wales. Enclosing £10, he made certain Kenneth knew that, '…*althou you are retired you are not forgotten*'.

At some stage in the late 1930s, Kenneth went back to work for English Electric which had taken over the Dick Kerr Works in Preston. Once again he picked up another positive testimonial to take with him to the next job, work at the much respected Imperial Chemical Industries (ICI) Huddersfield.

As you look at the photograph, Kenneth is fifth from the left in the second row from the front. They seem a happy bunch.

From ICI Huddersfield he moved further north to Teesside. Just months before the start of World War II, in July 1939, Kenneth applied successfully for a job as a welder with ICI Billingham. This section of ICI specialised in making fertilizers and synthetic products. It could sound innocuous – fertilizers and synthetic products – but as time went on, Kenneth was to realise that these things were not always that benign.

Meanwhile, back in Wales

After Kenneth left home, Frank settled into his new home with his three daughters and the latest housekeeper. Third time lucky you might think with the housekeeper. Frank certainly seemed to think so as in early 1930, and somewhat out of the blue, he married this one: May Hopley, otherwise known as Mabel Inez Hopley, a widow. May was the daughter of Charles William Gorey (deceased), an inspector of customs. The wedding took place in the Registry Office in Llanelli. Frank's daughter, Isabel, and her sister-in-law, Lilian, were the witnesses.

I was intrigued at May/Mabel's middle name which sounds to be Spanish. I tried all sorts of census, birth and marriage searches to see when she had married Mr Hopley and where she and her family had lived but drew a complete blank. With assistance from my cousin, Pauline, who by now was also hooked on the mystery of Mabel, we tracked down some information on various ancestry websites. 'Our' Mabel was living in Hastings, but not Hastings in Sussex – Hastings in Calcutta. No wonder that we could not find anything of her and her family in the UK! Her first husband, Percy Francis Hopley was, like Mabel's father, a customs officer, but in Calcutta. Mabel and Percy were married in St Stephen's Church in Kidderpore, Calcutta on 16 April 1895.

For whatever reason, Mabel's first marriage seems not to have lasted because, in 1911, Percy became the father of a son to one Margaret Amelia Fox. At some stage, Mabel had come back to the UK but why she should turn up in South Wales is still a mystery. She was living at 26 Graig Park Circle, Newport when she married my grandfather in the Llanelli registry office. It was not long before she returned to Newport. After a blazing row, she left. She then tried to take Frank to court to claim maintenance off him. She did not win her case as the taxi driver who took her and her suitcases to Llanelli station heard her say to Frank, *'I am leaving you and I am not coming back'*. The taxi driver stood as witness for Frank and her claim was dismissed.

The mysterious May/Mabel continues to be elusive. I can find no record of her having remarried, nor have I found her death for certain (or the death of her first husband). In fact I can't even be sure that she was a widow when she married Frank. Perhaps this was the cause of the row.

After the May/Mabel experience, Frank appeared to have given up on housekeepers. Isabel, Violet and Vera looked after themselves, their father and the home. Vera, at 9 or 10 years of age, was considered old enough to look after herself. This was just as well as her father was out at work and her elder sisters were both working full time at Woolworth's in Vaughan Street, Llanelli. Having jobs in shops, restaurants, offices and factories was considered far better than domestic work of any kind and was much better paid. Weekly wages were of the order of thirty shillings (£1.50) or £2 in the 1930s. The Lewis girls worked at Woolworth's at the same time as Edna May Squires. Edna May later became Dorothy Squires, one of the most popular singing stars of the 1940s.

Woolworth's was a household name by the early 1920s. The American store had taken Britain by storm. In its heyday, Woolworth opened a new place every 17 days, translating the American 5 and 10 cents offer into three old pence (3d) and six old pence (6d) for British shoppers. Their construction workers were known to be able to put up a store on a brownfield site in just seven weeks.

Permission to open the store in Llanelli had been granted by the local council in July 1927. Opening day at a Woolworth's store was an exciting affair attracting hundreds. Bands, fireworks, flags and bunting all promoted a great razzmatazz. The store became a focal point in the town, known by its trademark dark-red banner bearing the name of F W Woolworth & Co. Ltd. over the shop front and its promise that nothing would cost more than sixpence (6d).

The Lewis girls were well known and liked in Woolworth's as thoroughly modern misses. Both loved working in the store, competing with one another as to who was serving on the best counter. The 'best' counters in their eyes were those where they could chat to eligible young men as they served them. In practice, the counter girls were moved around the store to see if they were suited to be supervisors. Isabel said she never became a supervisor as she was not sharp enough to stop wily customers pilfering from her counter at busy times.

Like all the counter girls, Isabel and Vi were smartly dressed in a maroon uniform (that looked a bit like a gym slip) and black shoes with a small heel. Woolworth's sales staff had to be in the store dressed in their uniform by 8.45am. At this time the store manager inspected the staff and their counters a quarter of an hour before the store opened. Everything had to be neat and tidy.

Selling at the counters was seen as girls' work. Men worked in stock control and were paid more. In between serving customers, the counter girls made lists of items they had sold. The girls gave their lists to the stock men who toured the store with items to replenish those sold. The counters had to look as though they were fully stocked.

At lunchtime, which started on a rota any time from 11.00am, the girls and stock men could eat a subsidised hot meal in the staff canteen. After lunch, things were generally quiet until about 3.00pm, when mothers came in with their children. The end of the week was the busiest time when people had their weekly wages.

The counter girls worked a five and a half day week with one afternoon off during the week as well as Sunday. The half-day-closing day was the same in any given town and was usually a quieter day: Tuesday, Wednesday, or Thursday. In Llanelli, it was Tuesday.

If the girls married, they were given a combined wedding and leaving present and rarely came back to work.

People could buy all sorts of modern things at Woolworth's for a few pennies. The store even made it easy on the purse by selling things like a saucepan and its lid as separate items. You could buy clothes (and the wool to knit your own things), household goods, stationery, toys and, of course, sweets that were weighed out to suit the customer's needs. Things like records came into their own in the 1920s and 1930s. Children's songs like The Laughing Policeman were popular as were songs that were to become classics such as Smoke Gets in Your Eyes.

One week, Isabel used some of her wages to make a bathing costume out of something called Swimwell wool purchased, of course, at Woolworth's. At this time she was courting Eric, her husband to be, and one Sunday they had gone cycling to Gower. Stopping on Llangennith beach, she proudly went into the water in her newly knitted bathing costume. When she stood up in the sea, Eric immediately pushed her back into the water. The weight of the water had stretched the swimming garment so much that it was pouched around her waist exposing her top half. So much for Swimwell wool!

Isabel in her knitted swimsuit.

Around this time, Isabel had a short holiday with her older brother Denton and his wife, Lilian. Using the huge sum of five shillings from her wages, she joined the ranks of the bright young things who thought they were Amelia Earhart or Amy Johnson. She went up in an aeroplane for a joy ride. The plane was open to the atmosphere and the rush of air made it impossible to speak or to hear what someone else was saying. I am sure that nowadays there would be some European Directive preventing such a daredevil escapade. But in

Isabel in her 20s.

the early 1930s, for ten whole minutes, as she swooped down to land in a field, narrowly missing the tops of the hedges, she was a pioneer of flight.

Vi in her 20s. She and Isabel must have had the same hairdresser.

Other popular pastimes in the 30s were hiking and cycling. Getting out of smoke-filled towns and cities into the countryside beyond on foot or on cycles became relatively cheap and exhilarating pastimes. Isabel and her husband to be, Eric James, were up with the trend and became keen cyclists and ramblers on Gower. The sense of freedom and getting away from overcrowded houses must have been a big lure. Dressed in her men's shirt and shorts with an elasticated belt, Isabel looked every bit the modern young woman. Thinking back to her grandmother's day of only 20 years before, when not even an ankle was on display, these clothes and exploits must have been seen as very daring indeed.

Isabel the hiker.

Having courted Eric for a decent amount of time for him to be deemed acceptable to her family, Isabel married her beau in 1932. Her sisters Vi and Vera were the adult bridesmaids. Her brother Denton's young daughter Ursula and one of Eric's young nieces were the child bridesmaids. Isabel was proudly taken up the aisle by her father, Frank. More formal than anyone else at the wedding in his double breasted morning coat, high collars, white bow tie, sporting a waxed moustache, our Frank looked like an extra from a scene in 'Downton Abbey'.

Prominent by his absence was Kenneth. He was far away working in Scotland at the time. He always said he was viewed as the black sheep for not returning home for the occasion. His sister Isabel clearly held no animosity about his absence as she always regarded Kenneth as her favourite brother.

Isabel and Eric's wedding 1932.

Six years later, Kenneth's youngest sister Vera married Harry Davies, a well-known character in Carmarthen. Vera and her husband lived in Abergwili with her father, Frank, and unmarried sister, Vi. Both of Vera's children, Brian and Tony, were born there. They lived in what used to be the White Ox public house, by then number 6 High Street.

On New Year's Day 1940, Frank wrote to Kenneth and Elsie wishing them (in English and in Welsh) a Happy New Year. It is a warm and demonstrative letter addressed *'My Dear Son and Daughter'* and signed *'from your loving and affectionate Dad and sisters'* with eight kisses. He says that he and Violet had been thinking about Kenneth and Mickey (my father's nickname for Elsie) on New Year's Eve. The letter is written in a neat hand and with more attention to spelling and grammar than one might expect from a boy who had left school by the age of 12. Its style echoes those letters he wrote from the front in South Africa.

In the letter, Frank talks about his work and its effect on his health. He describes the freezing cold weather and treacherous roads. He reflects on the war and his desire for peace. Slipping into something of a Churchillian mode he hopes the year, *'…will be a prosperous one although it is clouded by the dark storm clouds of war let us pray God will give us the victory or we will be slaves for ever…'*

Frank's letter shows that, aged 70, he was still working full time in the Glanmor Foundry in Llanelli. In fact he describes how he had worked late each day throughout the Christmas period, including Christmas Day and Boxing Day. At the time of writing he was very unwell suffering from, *'…a poisoned stomach and chest'*. He talks of the pressure on his heart, ascribing his illness to having to go into the *'…Black Hole of a Boiler House which heats the offices'*. He writes of the awful fumes from the boiler and of nearly being overcome with carbon monoxide.

A week later, on Monday 8 January 1940, and by now off work ill, Frank wrote a letter to his daughter Isabel and Eric who were living in Llanelli. The letter acknowledged receipt of the pay that Eric had picked up from the works on Frank's behalf. In the letter, he reveals that he has been working about 80 hours a week in the foundry. He describes his health as having broken down and says that there is very little likelihood of his returning to work under the same circumstances. He advises Eric to go to the foundry and ask if he can have Frank's job. He shows great concern (*'…listen to your Old Dad…'*) for his son-in-law, especially for the fact that Eric is out working in all weathers. He says that Eric should look for work where he will be inside and out of the cold and rain, adding that there will be plenty of vacancies for burners and welders as younger men are being called up in their thousands to serve in the war.

After returning home from walking to the post-box with the letter that afternoon, Frank sat down to read one of his favourite Edgar Wallace thrillers. A short while later, he had a heart attack and died.

Frank's eldest son, Denton, was present at his father's death. He took over the arrangements of the funeral and the dividing up of his father's estate.

My father kept the papers drawn up by Denton to share out the estate amongst Frank's five children. Each account was produced on tissue thin paper and copies sent to the brothers and sisters. Each was headed 'Kenneth's share', 'Isabel's share', and so on. The accounts show, amongst other attributes, the meticulous nature of his elder brother. He had calculated all of the sums to the nearest halfpenny and, probably, typed up the accounts in a quiet moment in the police station where he was based.

The house in Abergwili was sold for around £320, similar to about £9,100 nowadays. Various life insurance policies were cashed in to the sum of about £90, equating to over £2,500 in today's value. The contents of the house were sold right down to the dustbin, and the receipts totted up. Family members and neighbours were charged the going rate for items sold off. Even the eggs that the hens had laid in the interim were sold and accounted for. It is not clear what happened to the hens!

I thought that it was harsh to charge Vera for things that were, after all, part of her home too, especially as the sale of the house in Abergwili made her homeless. Vera was four months pregnant, homeless because of the death of her father, coping with her two year old son who had been ill, with a husband who was about to leave the area for the army, and her elder brother actually took money off her for a table and a bit of linoleum. Kenneth could not believe the detail of his brother's accounts.

The costs associated with the sale of the house and the funeral were similarly and scrupulously shared amongst each of the brothers and sisters, right down to the last halfpenny for bread, cakes and meat for the funeral tea. When all was settled, the two brothers and three sisters each received a sum of just under £60, worth about £1,800 in value today. Although this might not sound much, bearing in mind what people earned at that time, that sum would have been about half a year's wages.

Frank's death and funeral made the local papers as a news item. One report featured a photograph of Frank looking smart in his uniform as commissionaire at the foundry. He was well known and well regarded for his army and police service and for his work in the foundry. The whole family was at the funeral including Kenneth who had come down from Teesside, his first visit home since he had left Wales in the late 1920s. High-ranking police officers, the local JP and senior managers of the Glanmor Foundry also turned out. Some 70 police officers (described as a 'posse' by one newspaper) from the Carmarthenshire Constabulary under the command of the Deputy Chief Constable headed the cortege as it proceeded the short distance from the High Street to Abergwili

Parish Church where Frank had married Mary Francis nearly forty years before. Frank was buried in the churchyard there not far from other generations of Lewis ancestors.

Frank died when the Second World War had barely started. A staunch Conservative and patriot, he would stand up every time the National Anthem was played. He even stood up if there was a royal broadcast on the radio. He believed in Britain being invincible and, like many others in late 1939, thought that the war would be soon over. After seeing an air raid shelter being built in Llanelli railway station grounds, he had remarked that, '...*they (the Germans) would never come over here*'. Fortunately he never lived to know about the bombing of Britain and food rationing, nor of what happened to his daughter-in-law (Elsie, my mother) and grandson (Tony, my brother) in 1941.

Work, war and survival

As he made the long, cold train journey back to Teesside after his father's funeral, Kenneth had plenty of time to contemplate the years since he had first left Wales. That winter was one of the longest, coldest and snowiest on record. Temperatures of -21 degrees C were recorded in parts of England and snow, measured in feet, disrupted train travel and made life even more miserable as the war and its effects at home began to bite.

Far from making him homesick for Wales, Kenneth's visit to Wales made him feel relieved to be going to what he now thought of as home, the newly rented house at 6 Malden Road, Norton, which he shared with Elsie. He was delighted to have his job as an electric welder at ICI, a firm known for its good employment conditions. Although he did not know it, his wandering days were over and he was to stay with ICI for over 30 years.

Kenneth had landed on his feet by gaining employment at ICI. By the 1930s, ICI was the largest factory in the British Empire with a fine reputation for its terms and conditions of employment. The plant in Billingham had grown after the First World War because of the actions of another man of Welsh descent, David Lloyd George (no, he did not know my father!). The Welsh-speaking Manchester-born politician had highlighted a key manufacturing supply problem that had occurred in the 1914-1918 war. Britain did not have home access to a source of nitrogen to make the explosive trinitrotoluene (TNT). During the First World War, Britain had to rely on importing nitrates from Chile for this purpose while Germany had access to its own local supply. It was not long before German U-boats attacked the nitrate-bearing ships from Chile. In a 'never again' moment, Lloyd George asked the Ministry responsible to set up an organisation in Britain which could produce synthetic ammonia as a nitrogen source for making explosives. Brunner Mond & Co from Cheshire was selected to carry out the work and chose the site at Billingham for that development. As a site, Billingham was ideal as it had ready access to coal, water and power. It may also have been a partly political choice. ICI went on to provide work for the many unemployed shipyard workers in that area of the North East from 1926 onwards. The first synthetic ammonia (Synthonia) produced by the factory did not emerge until the First World War was long over and then it was mainly used in the manufacture of nitrogenous fertilisers.

ICI continued to grow and diversify making oil from coal and various kinds of plastics including Perspex. At the outbreak of the Second World War, therefore, Billingham had a key role to play in manufacturing many chemicals and products that were vital in fighting the war.

Kenneth, in his thirties, when the Second World War broke out, was of an age to have been called up for armed service. However, his work in ICI was judged as essential to the war effort. In other words, he was in a reserved occupation. The government was determined not to make the mistake it had done during the First World War when so many men were conscripted into the armed forces that essential non-military work was short of the necessary workforce.

Kenneth worked in a number of sections in ICI: with the external platers in the Engineering Works; in Oil Works; and later in Casebournes. His work took him outdoors in all weathers. It took him inside in conditions of such heat that would not be allowed nowadays because of health and safety. Time to shut down plant and allow it to cool down was time lost in manufacturing. Essential maintenance work or fixing breakdowns was expected to go on as quickly as possible.

Throughout the war, as a fit and strong-looking man, Kenneth was often asked, usually by women, why he wasn't in the army. He would reply that his occupation was reserved, but that did not stop the sceptical looks from those whose husbands and brothers had been called up. Fed up with being taunted in this way, he went to the army recruiting office in Stockton and tried to join the Royal Engineers, only to be told that they could not take him because of his work. When he went back a further time, the recruiting officer told him to *'bugger off'* and stop wasting their time. He asked the recruiting staff if they would give him a letter that he could show anyone who asked so as to stop the insults.

Keen to carry out some visible war effort outside of his paid work,

Kenneth volunteered as a 'special' doing air-raid duty with his friend Dick Ramage, manager of Boots the Chemist in Stockton. Their duties included going out when the air raid sirens sounded to make sure that people had followed the advised routine to prevent the German bomber flights being able to see lights on the ground below. Our house in Billingham had marks all around the window frames from the drawing pins that had held the blackout material in place at the windows. During a blackout, there were no street lights and motor vehicles had special headlamps that gave out little light. Being out during these times was dangerous and even though lampposts and the edges of pavements were painted white or with luminous paint, there were many accidents through collisions, trips and falls. People received hefty fines if they shone a light outside or left on house lights without adequately covering their windows during an air raid. There were even reports of men receiving prison sentences with hard labour for using lights during a blackout.

From mid-summer 1940 to spring 1943, attacks rained down on the whole of the North East from Humberside to Tyneside. Elsie's mind must have often turned to Hull which was particularly badly bombed. For example, at the end of August and beginning of September 1941, a direct hit there on a civilian shelter caused many casualties. About 200 homes were demolished or damaged, and thirty-eight people were killed.

The North East was a prime target for German air strikes because of the work in heavy manufacturing industries. The walls and roofs of the buildings in the factory at ICI Billingham were covered in camouflage paint to make them look like the countryside to German bombers overhead. They stayed in this state long after the war. I can recall the cooling towers and some of the administrative buildings bearing their brown and green paint well into the 1950s.

In late 1940, some decoy sites were set up around Billingham to draw bombing away from the ICI and other strategically important factories. On these decoy sites, fires and explosions were deliberately started and lights placed tactically to simulate factories and ammunition dumps working under blackout conditions. The sites were usually in open fields away from the real target and drew over 200 attacks by German bombers thinking they had found their industrial targets.

Incendiary bombs and high explosives intended for ICI sometimes fell instead on homes nearby. It is hard to imagine how tired and frightened people would have been with the relentless attacks night after night. Scores of bombs were dropped on houses, damaging property, gas and water mains and making people homeless. The worst of these raids killed and injured people. Kenneth reported finding body parts of people at a considerable distance from where the bombs had fallen.

For about 18 months from mid-1940 to late 1941, the German attackers seemed to find their position on Teesside. ICI and some of the surrounding areas were occasionally hit causing fires and explosions that could be made more lethal because of the chemicals and inflammables in the target sites.

On Sunday 11 to Monday 12 May 1941, ICI at Billingham was attacked by nineteen enemy aircraft between 00.30 and 02.10. The aircraft dropped twenty-seven tons of high explosive (twenty-five bombs) and 1,584 incendiary devices.

The following month King George VI and Queen Elizabeth made a morale-boosting tour of the North East, including a visit to Billingham, to see factories, meet people and appreciate the war damage.

Overnight on 17 to 18 August 1941, bombs were reported in Norton-on-Tees. In these frightening circumstances, Elsie gave birth on 18 August to Anthony William Lewis, Kenneth's and her first child.

Although they could not have known this at the time, Tony's birth was to make sure that Elsie was never conscripted into a war-related job. In December 1941, an Act of Parliament was passed that required unmarried women aged between 20 and 30 to be called up. As a consequence of this Act, Kenneth's unmarried sister Vi had left her job in Woolworths and joined the Navy, Army and Air Force Institutes (NAAFI), an organisation that provided retail, leisure and catering services for Britain's Armed Forces around the world. In the event, I don't think that Vi travelled any further than Pembrokeshire. As the war continued, married women were made liable to be directed into war-related civilian work, although pregnant women and mothers with young children were completely exempt.

On the night of Monday 18 August and the early hours of 19 August 1941, the North East had an even worse night. A high explosive device fell near Cowpen Bewley Village and damaged twenty houses. A similar device, dropped a mile east of Billingham railway station near to the main Stockton to West Hartlepool line, caused damage to the line and equipment and damaged a railway house.

In the early hours of 19 August 1941 in nearby Norton, just hours after my brother had been born in Malden Road, a bomb fell nearby between Benson Street and Pine Street causing considerable damage. At least seven people were killed or missing and twenty-one were seriously injured. Approximately twenty people were made homeless, amongst them Kenneth, Elsie and their new baby boy.

Kenneth was out of the house at the time of the blast, carrying out air-raid warden duties. He returned home to the shock of finding his own house badly damaged. There was serious damage to every room in the place apart from the room where Elsie was with baby Tony.

The newly-born Tony was wrapped up in a blanket in a Moses basket that Elsie had pushed under the bed when the explosions started. The midwife burst into tears when she saw the dust-covered baby in the basket, thinking he had been killed by the blast. Miraculously, neither he nor Elsie was injured. Within a few weeks, Kenneth and Elsie found a house for rent about a mile away in Billingham on a large estate built and owned then by ICI.

The bombing in the area continued. If anything, Kenneth and family were now closer to it in Billingham. The German bombers kept up their attacks on ICI and some of the surrounding houses and buildings. Fires were a frequent consequence of the bombing and some of the men, including Kenneth, acted as firemen. Kenneth continued in this role long after the war ended as fires were not uncommon in the factory. He was commended for this work by the Chairman of ICI in a letter thanking him for his service when he had reached the milestone of 20 years with the company.

The services of firemen were needed overnight on Monday 6 and Tuesday 7 July 1942. The North East area was bombed by a large number of enemy aircraft. ICI at Billingham was hit with high explosives and incendiary devices which caused seventeen fires in under an hour. An oil tank that received a direct hit lost a million gallons of petrol. A fireman was killed and six others were injured. Houses on the surrounding estate were damaged and some destroyed.

The following day the bombers were back again causing more fires in ICI, deaths and injuries to workers and householders, together with damage to property including schools, a church, houses and commercial buildings. Many families had to be evacuated and rehomed.

By the end of the war, some 15 people in Billingham had been killed and a further 70 or so injured.

In the late 1930s, the UK imported about two thirds of all its food. As an island nation, we depended on ships to bring us many of the foodstuffs that we had grown to love and expect in our diet. With hostile German ships and aircraft on the lookout for merchant ships coming to Britain, it was clear that things had to change. Rationing of food started on the day that Frank had died: 8 January 1940. First bacon, butter and sugar were rationed, followed by meat, tea, margarine, jam, breakfast cereals, biscuits, cheese, eggs, lard, milk and canned and dried fruits To be issued with a ration book, everyone first had to obtain a national identity card. Once you had your identity card, and my father regarded this as sufficiently important to keep it all his life, you were issued with a ration book. The ration books for all members of the family had to be taken to the shops each week to have the stamps in them cancelled in exchange for the various rationed commodities.

A person's typical weekly allowance would be: one fresh egg; 4oz margarine, cooking fat and bacon (about four rashers); 2oz butter and tea; 1oz cheese; and 8oz sugar. Meat was allocated by price (to the value of one shilling and sixpence) therefore cheaper cuts became popular. Points could be pooled or saved to buy other goods such as pulses, cereals, tinned goods, dried fruit, biscuits and jam. Wasting food became a criminal offence. Typing those words makes awkward reading in the era of sell-by and use-by dates on food products. People then used their sight, smell and taste, to judge if something was still edible. Research done in 2011 in Britain showed that families threw away on average about £680 worth of food per year, amounting to a massive £12 billion worth of food going to waste in the country as a whole.

The 'dig for victory' campaign had started almost as soon as war was declared and by 1943, millions of tons of food were being harvested from gardens and allotments up and down the land. Spare land in parks and open spaces was converted into vegetable patches to broaden people's diets beyond the limits of the ration book. Kenneth and Elsie did their bit by growing produce such as blackcurrants, blackberries, gooseberries and potatoes in their garden in Stokesley Crescent, Billingham.

Elsie was an accomplished cook, seamstress and gardener. She had some cookery books from the 1930s and earlier. The ones that have survived are: Universal Cookery Book published by W Foulsham; a volume entitled Cookery for the Middle Classes by Miss Tuxford; and Elizabeth Craig's Economical Cookery. The Universal Cookery Book was probably the oldest of the books, possibly late Victorian or Edwardian, as it talks of cooking over a fire. Amongst the 1,000 recipes in the Universal Cookery Book were ones for prune marmalade (*...take 3lbs of prunes...*), travellers' sandwiches (containing cooked lentils and cheese...) and jugged hare (*...clean and wash the hare...*). The middle class cookery book, which was in its twelfth edition, was priced 1 shilling. For this sum of money you received, *'720 well tried and economical recipes'*. The book contained, *'useful hints on gas stove cooking, including the new automatic control'*. Recipes ranged from the sublime, like how to make grilled chop a la maître d'hôtel, to the ridiculous, such as how to boil potatoes!

Many of the recipes in these books would have looked positively extravagant by the 1940s. The ingredients required for a simple pudding would either have been unavailable or else would have gobbled up a lot of the weekly rations for several people in one go. I can imagine that by 1940 Elsie would have turned to her third cookery book, Elizabeth Craig's Economical Cookery. In there was a section called, Hints on Catering and Cooking in War-Time. The hints included eking out the butter ration by combining it with milk, cornflour and salt and allowing it to re-set. There were detailed instructions for drying, bottling and pickling the fruits of one's labours in the garden or allotment. The author even had helpful advice on how to save coal, gas and electricity by cooking with a hay box, something I had thought was confined to scouts' and girl guides' repertoires. To round off the book, she had six emergency war-time recipes including one for making bread out of flour and potatoes, one for making sugarless date jam, and one for a cake that was eggless and fatless. How about having a go at those on the Great British Bake Off!

As well as food being rationed, so too were household goods and commodities we take for granted such as soap, fuel and paper. Even well into the 1950s, paper was in short supply. Kenneth used to bring home from work waste paper he had pulled out of the bins. The paper had only been printed on one side and my brother and I used to write and draw on the unused side.

As rationing kicked in, Kenneth realised that the family diet would be low on meat. The solution was to keep and fatten up some sort of animal. Many people kept chickens or clubbed together to keep a pig. Kenneth decided with his friend Dick Ramage that they would each keep and breed rabbits. They kept fancy ones like chinchillas. These animals had the dual benefit that they could be both eaten and supply an income to pay for their feed from the sale of their pelts. Kenneth cured some of the pelts himself with saltpetre. This was not always a great success. I remember, all too well, the skins remaining too stiff for ease of movement whilst wearing the home-made gloves. He sent the best pelts to a firm called Waddington's in Hull to be cured professionally. He continued breeding rabbits long after the war ended as rationing of meat did not end until 1954. Kenneth would tell the tale of being offered a rabbit by Dick as they chatted over a pint in the Red Lion pub in Norton. It seems that Dick did not want the large sable rabbit as it was too aggressive for breeding. Never one to look a gift horse in the mouth, especially when it was a rabbit, Kenneth took possession of said animal. The rabbit instantly showed its credentials by thrashing this way and that in the sack on its way home. It set upon Elsie each time she tried to feed it. It drew blood and loud squeals from the dog next door as it came sniffing at the rabbit's cage. All were agreed that this situation could not continue. The rabbit was killed and dressed for the table. It weighed in at around nine pounds and provided the family with a roast dinner, a pie and a stew.

Whilst people managed the austerity and rationing through make-do-and-mend and creative cookery, there were people who took advantage of the shortages in food and clothing by operating a black market in scarce goods. If they were caught, the law came down hard on such people. A wholesale fruiterer in Middlesbrough was fined £600 and sentenced to six months hard labour in prison for selling over a hundred crates of apples for four shillings a crate above the controlled price. Hard labour probably meant the man concerned spending each day of his sentence breaking up stones with a sledge hammer so that the stone was small enough to be used in road making, but few would have felt sympathy for him.

One day, in the early 1940s, there was a knock on the door of Kenneth and Elsie's home in Billingham. To Kenneth's astonishment, there, dressed in his army uniform, stood his youngest sister's husband, Harry Davies. Harry had gone AWOL from his posting in Catterick. After Elsie gave him a meal (*'...there's tender the gravy is!'* became a family catchphrase), Kenneth saved Harry from being court marshalled by taking him back via several buses to Catterick. Although he was not court marshalled, he was punished with extra duties to deter him from disappearing again.

As the war dragged on, there was an increasing fear of aliens. No, not little green men from Mars, but foreigners, especially Germans, Austrians and Italians. Kenneth and Dick encountered at first hand the suspicion that existed amongst the population one weekend when they went out walking on the North Yorkshire Moors. During their walk, they had stopped for a drink in a local hostelry. Not long after leaving the public house, they were approached by an out-of-breath policeman on a bicycle who asked them to accompany him to the local police station. During the interview that followed, they were told that one of the locals had reported them thinking they might be German spies. They were picked up because they were strangers to the area and they did not speak with the same accents as the locals. Fortunately they were both carrying their identity cards and were allowed to go on their way.

Kenneth: North Yorks Moors in 1940s

Three months after the war in Europe had ended, Kenneth was called to do some work in a part of ICI he had never visited. He and two other welders were taken to this place and each given a separate part of the metal plant to burn down. By burn down, I mean cut up sections of the pipework using their welding and burning gear. Each section of pipework was placed in railway trucks that were standing by to take it away. By the time the three welders were finished, there was no trace that this plant had ever existed. Their work took place just after the bombing of Hiroshima. The place where they had worked was known as Tube Alloys and was where some of the development work had been carried out for the atomic bomb.

War over, austerity continues, but work prospers

Growing up in the 50s and 60s, it seemed to me as though everything was defined by whether it was before or after the war. In domestic terms, the effects of war carried on long after the hostilities ended. Rationing did not stop completely until 4 July 1954: the last things to be freed being bacon and meat. In fact, rationing became worse before it got better as bread started to be rationed after the war in 1946 and potatoes were rationed in 1947.

But, working for ICI was proving to be a good move for Kenneth. He entered enthusiastically into all that was on offer from his employer. For a small weekly sum, he joined the Billingham Life Benefit Society which paid out the sum of £250 on his death over 50 years later. In 1947, he achieved something significant when he was accepted on staff grade. This meant that he had improved status at work, greater security in his employment and access to a guaranteed staff grade wage comprising the plain time rate, any personal allowance and a service bonus.

He also had to be given four weeks' notice if he was dismissed, a level of security never before experienced. To achieve this status he had to prove he was reliable, willing, trustworthy and able to exercise a good influence in the works. Once on this grade, he and his work was reviewed at regular intervals to make sure that he was continuing to show the qualities demanded by the scheme.

Life was on the up and the family was happy.

Kenneth playing on the beach with Tony late 1940s.

Kenneth planned ahead to his retirement, happily paying into the company pension scheme. In the mid-1950s, his contributions were deducted from his wages of at a rate of 2½%. In his eighties, after benefitting from the pension for over 21 years, he felt that this had been one of his better decisions in life. By the time he died in 1991, his weekly index-linked pension was more than twice what he had been paying in per year some 35 years before. When the sum was paid into his bank account every fortnight, he felt he had won the jackpot.

In 1954, ICI introduced a profit-sharing scheme. The purpose of this was to increase the number of employees who felt they had a direct interest in the financial affairs and success of the company. The scheme worked by annually awarding employees a bonus in the form of shares which could be kept or sold by the recipient. The amount received was based on the level of the worker's pay and the profitability of the company that year. During the 1950s, the stock acquired amounted to an additional annual sum worth two to four times Kenneth's weekly wages, depending on how well the company had done.

ICI was viewed as paternalistic by some but pay that was above the average for similar work in other factories, together with privileges and amenities provided to employees, certainly secured a loyal and fairly content workforce. Following in the footsteps of some of the great Victorian employers such as George Cadbury and Sir Titus Salt, ICI built houses for its workforce between the First and Second World Wars. Thousands of houses were provided in Billingham. There was a pecking order in the style and allocation of the houses. Some detached houses were reserved for senior managers in two roads off Billingham Bank and in Norton. Houses for the less senior managers were in Mill Lane and Malvern Road while the workers occupied the great many houses near to the factory in the estate to the east of Mill Lane and, more especially, in the estate north of Belasis Avenue where Kenneth and family lived. As far as Kenneth was concerned this house with three bedrooms, a bathroom, two living rooms downstairs and front and rear gardens was a modern place to live. ICI seemed constantly to be upgrading their stock in one way or another. For example, after the passing of the Clean Air Act (1954), all houses had their fireplaces replaced and new 'clean' coke burning fires installed. Another 'modernisation' in the 1960s was the flushing of all interior doors with hardboard panels and beading (see next photograph) and the replacing of round wooden door knobs with plastic handles and ball catch door closers. To this day I cannot imagine why dressing up the doors in this way was seen as such a priority.

The houses were eventually sold off to a property trust but only after ICI offered them to the sitting tenants at preferential rates. ICI even went so far as to offer to lend money to their employees for the purpose of buying the houses.

Kenneth's going-to-work attire consisted of an old pair of trousers, a khaki shirt over which he wore dark blue overalls and either an old jacket or a woollen navy donkey jacket. On his head he favoured a black beret and on his feet either a pair of rubber, steel-capped boots or an old pair of brown leather shoes with reinforced toes. Most of this gear could be ordered from a shop in ICI. Every few years, Kenneth would order a new pair of dark brown shoes with a steel toe cap. He would dance me round the room with my feet on his to show how solid the shoes were. Size 8: for a big chap, he had surprisingly small feet. The new shoes were worn initially for 'best' and the ones they replaced were then worn for going to work. ICI even supplied towels to workers and every so often we had a new supply of the creamy-white coloured towels with a green band down the middle showing through the initials ICI. Icky the Great Provider, as Kenneth called ICI!

For evenings and weekends, Kenneth wore either a dark navy blazer (spring to summer) or a tweed jacket (autumn to winter), both over wide-legged dark grey trousers (always referred to as flannels) with turn-ups. He would be fitted every now and then for new versions of these items in the Co-op on The Green. The new clothes would be ceremoniously brought home in a brown string-tied paper package. The paper and string would be carefully removed and stored pending re-use. The old trousers and jackets were then relegated to work wear.

Kenneth particularly liked checked shirts and always wore his shirt sleeves rolled up. He did not like wearing a tie although he always felt he should unless it was a warm summer evening – there might be one or two each year up on Teesside. Variations like a jumper (with or without sleeves), an overcoat or a raincoat (a Mac) and scarf and gloves could be introduced to suit the weather. A newer beret was usually in his pocket in case it rained. The beret was a bit of a trademark until well into the early 1980s. Then, when the IRA were in the news sporting their black berets, he was persuaded (for the avoidance of doubt) to wear a flat cap with a peak!

Kenneth in the renowned beret! If you look closely, you can see the edge of an ICI towel hanging up in the scullery and the famous door modernisation.

Like Cadbury did in the village of Bournville, in Birmingham, ICI also built a recreational club where employees could keep fit and relax by enjoying a range of sports including football, tennis and cricket. Unlike Cadbury, the Billingham Synthonia Recreation Club also had bars where employees and their guests could relax over a drink (or two). Kenneth, like many others, would often call in to the Club on his way home from work. After a hard shift in hot or dusty places, this was just the place to relax, rehydrate and refresh oneself before going home. At weekends, Club members could bring along their family and non-employees could become associate members. The Club had a theatre and other pastimes such as photography could be enjoyed. Trips, galas, dances, variety entertainment and outings added to the menu on offer via the Club which was very much a focal point in the community.

Sometime in the early 1950s, Kenneth did a spell as a committee man in the Synthonia Club. He also had something to do with running the football for Billingham Synthonia team (Synners). As a child, I recall being taken on a Saturday afternoon to watch the Synners play in their green and white strip on the Belasis Avenue pitch. However, I remember the bottle of lemonade and the bag of crisps I was given more than I do the football.

Kenneth's spell as a committee man did not last long. He was far too much of a free spirit to be sitting creating rules and regulations for others to follow. But the Club in one form or another was a large part of his life. He was a life member of both the Synthonia and the Billingham Social Club. Which entertainment was on offer, for example dominoes, dancing, music and variety acts, would determine which he would frequent.

The Synthonia Committee circa 1954 with Kenneth at the back, far right.

Kenneth told many a tale of personalities with whom he worked. They all seemed to have nicknames or characterful names, like George the Pole, All-night-Robbo, Eddie Chicken, and Chancellor Campbell. Two of his closest mates were Paddy Jarvis and Nobby Clark. Why Paddy (Walter) was so named is not clear, especially as he was not Irish. Nobby (Gowland) was in a long line of Nobby Clarks supposedly after a type of hat that used to be worn by clerks.

Kenneth always took sandwiches to work for his lunch. Occasionally he would exchange sandwiches with another worker. One day at work he was having his sandwiches with George the Pole. Kenneth agreed to trade one of his corned beef sandwiches for one of George's. Kenneth ate the fishy-tasting swap and enjoyed it, so much so that he asked what was in it so that he could buy some. 'Oh', says George, 'it is quite cheap, comes in a large tin and is called Kit-e-Kat.' What you might call a purrfect filling!

Kenneth first encountered All-night-Robbo when he worked overtime and Robbo (real name Jack Robinson) was asked to work as Kenneth's mate. It seemed that Jack had acquired his nickname whilst working in the platers' shed outside Oil Works. He had received a blow to the head whilst passing too close to a blacksmith's striker. The blow to the head stunned him and as people rushed to his aid, one man slapped his face and asked him, 'Are you alright Robbo?' On coming out of his dazed state Robbo said, 'All night, yes, I'll work all night!'

Kenneth was still a union member but not one who relished some of the ways of union men. He was fond of telling a tale of a local shop steward, a plumber by trade, who often had to attend management meetings to sort out local difficulties concerning particular jobs. One day, the shop steward was told that he could not proceed with a request about some job as the matter was in abeyance. Giving feedback to the men he represented, the shop steward said that they could not talk about the job as it was in a basin. The same man came back from a trip to the doctor as a result of very bad catarrh. He told his mates that he had the guitar in his nose for which he had been prescribed menthol crystals which he had to place in hot water and ignore with a towel over his head!

As well as supplying housing in which the worker and a family could continue to live after retirement and a Club for sport and recreation,

ICI provided medical, dental and physiotherapy services via an on-site centre. The medical centre was located in the creeper-covered former farmhouse called the Grange. If someone was hurt or became ill at work, they were taken to the Grange for treatment. Chancellor Campbell was a rigger and by Kenneth's accounts a very good one. The riggers did dangerous work and one day Chancellor was taken to the medical room after a wire hawser struck him on the nose causing a nasty gash. The doctor on duty made a rather rough job of stitching Chancellor's nose which healed with an unsightly scar. Sometime later, poor Chancellor had the misfortune to suffer a similar accident and had to go to have his nose fixed once more. The same doctor was on duty and, taking one look at Chancellor's nose, he commented on the fact that it had been stitched before and not very expertly. Chancellor took no time in telling him that he was the so-and-so who had done it!

From the end of October 1955 until he retired in 1970, Kenneth worked at Casebourne Works or Cement Plant as it later became known. He smelled of cement when he came in from work. If I gave him a hug when he arrived home, I would be covered in a film of cement dust. The cement made in Casebourne's was packed into thick paper bags and loaded onto lorries for onward transport. Kenneth was much amused by the drivers who came in insisting on having one particular make of cement as opposed to another as the only thing that changed was the logo on the paper bag – all of the cement came out of the same chute.

During Kenneth's time at Casebourne's he reached 20 and then 30 years' service. Such things were marked with some ceremony and style at ICI. Kenneth kept the letters he received from the Chairman of the Board of ICI and the Chairman of the local division in Billingham. Workers could choose a clock or a watch to mark the occasion: a silver one for 20 years and a gold one for 30 years. Kenneth chose a watch in each case but he only ever wore the silver one. The watches were suitably engraved and presented at a dinner along with a certificate. ICI paternalism even extended to paying for any watch repairs and servicing that might be needed long after the award.

Who do you think they were?

How do you learn what people are really like? Ultimately they seem to be only what we think of them. Taking this tour amongst my ancestors has brought me face-to-face with five generations of Lewises and their immediate families. I have thought hard about how much of the preceding four generations was handed on to the one I knew at first hand, Kenneth. I think boldness and bravery would be high on the agenda in relation to all of them.

When Kenneth died, my brother and I placed announcements in the local papers in South Wales where he died and in the North East where he had lived for well over half of his life and where he was laid to rest. We said, '...*he was bold and brave and we are proud of him...*'

I also think that the gene for working hard must have been transferred to him from the preceding generations of men and women who worked almost up to the date when a final illness swiftly overtook them. Kenneth had a good reputation for the quality of his work and was well respected by those with whom he worked. As a teenager in Billingham, I can recall being asked in the village if I was 'Taff' Lewis' daughter. When I replied that I was, I was told he was a bloody good welder and a good man to work with. Kenneth had retired from ICI a year early because of ill health but, unlike his grandfather, he was fortunate to live at a time when medical advances helped him overcome the causes of his ill health. He survived serious chest infections, repeated bouts of pneumonia and major abdominal surgery to live to the age of 86. Any one of these conditions would have killed previous generations.

Kenneth regarded himself as a free spirit. He did not subscribe to any religious denomination. Being made to go to church three times on Sunday as a boy had the opposite effect to the one intended. He nevertheless held firm principles. He had flirted with humanism but even that was too much like a sect. He felt that an individual should be able to pursue his or her course of action but with the proviso that no one else was harmed and that the consequences of any action, whether wise or foolish, right or wrong, were accepted unequivocally. He was a man who looked for justice, integrity, honesty and modesty in all his dealings.

He was a quiet man with a dry sense of humour, a bit of an observer of those around him. Generous and charming, he was a leader who could calmly put others in their place if they were being uncouth or rude, especially if they were in the earshot of women and children. A heavy drinker himself in his heyday, he would nevertheless remain in charge of his language and behaviour. I remember him bringing home a neighbour who was the worse for drink. The neighbour's wife received the swaying husband with the words, *'He can't take it like you can, Lewis!'*

Kenneth had a sharp mind and a prodigious if rather esoteric knowledge base. What he knew was not acquired through formal education but from his travels and his avid reading of fiction and non-fiction books, mainly from the local library. He loved to read adventure and wildlife stories, particularly those about America, Australia and South Africa. Special favourites were the novels of Arthur Upfield featuring Bony (Detective Inspector Napoleon Bonaparte) the half-Aboriginal detective. He also liked Wilbur Smith's novels set in South Africa, no doubt prompted by listening to his father's tales of the place. I think if things had been different, we might have emigrated on the £10 passage to Australia in the 1960s as so many did from the North East, but he was not one to be regretful for things that had not come about.

I remember him once trying to learn to speak and write Esperanto, an artificially created language, the rudiments of which were in an annex in his much loved dictionary. One of the aims of the creator of Esperanto was to create an easy-to-learn and politically-neutral language that transcended nationality and would foster peace and international understanding between people with different regional and/or national languages. That appealed to him. He was not sentimental about his country of origin. Not one for 'hiraeth' or misty-eyed nostalgia. He lived where he was, in the moment as we might say now. He made the most of things rather than longed for things to be different. If he wanted things to be different then he felt it was up to him to make them so, but he did want the best for my brother and I, making no difference between us as far as ambition and support were concerned.

I see Kenneth as a blend of the principles of John, his great great grandfather, but with the spirit of his great grandfather, William, the 74 year old cattle drover-cum-publican. Kenneth's need to look for work wherever it could be found probably came from all of them but particularly from his grandfather, Francis, and his father William Francis, both of whom worked right up to their deaths.

How much of all of these Lewis traits there are in the younger branches of the family, only time will tell. And, of course, what we cannot know is the extent to which the non-Lewises contributed to our genetic make-up and personalities. But, the diagonal ties between the two opposite ends of the country must have strengthened us by widening our gene pool.

Acknowledgements

Thank you to kind friends who have helped in checking the manuscript in part or as a whole. Particular thanks go to Shan for wading through the whole book and, as always, making such useful suggestions. Thank you to Dale for checking the part about Witton Park and sharing his passion for the place and its history. Thank you to Davy for checking the sections where I talk about the iron industry.

Thank you to Llanelli Reference Library for their can-do attitude and help.

Having given those thanks, I would add that any errors, of whatever kind, are mine.

Extracts from the Lewis family tree

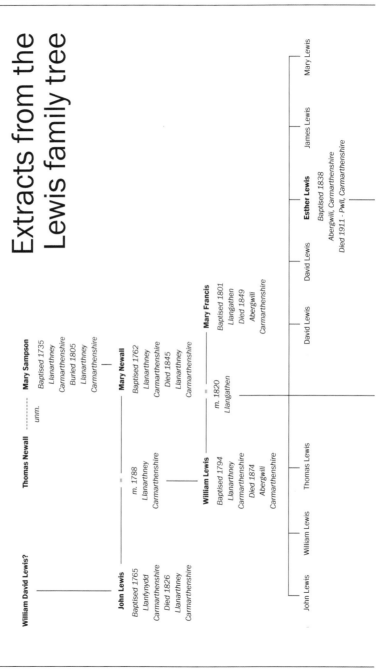

William David Lewis?

Thomas Newall -------- **Mary Sampson**
unm.
Baptised 1735
Llanarthney
Carmarthenshire
Buried 1805
Llanarthney
Carmarthenshire

John Lewis
Baptised 1765
Llanfynydd
Carmarthenshire
Died 1826
Llanarthney
Carmarthenshire

m. 1788
Llanarthney
Carmarthenshire

Mary Newall
Baptised 1762
Llanarthney
Carmarthenshire
Died 1845
Llanarthney
Carmarthenshire

William Lewis
Baptised 1794
Llanarthney
Carmarthenshire
Died 1874
Abergwili
Carmarthenshire

m. 1820
Llangathen

Mary Francis
Baptised 1801
Llangathen
Died 1849
Abergwili
Carmarthenshire

John Lewis   William Lewis   Thomas Lewis   David Lewis   David Lewis   **Esther Lewis**
Baptised 1838
Abergwili, Carmarthenshire
Died 1911 - Pwll, Carmarthenshire
James Lewis   Mary Lewis

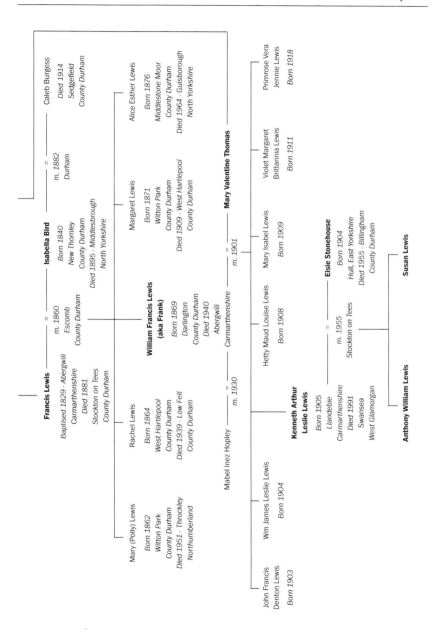

Francis Lewis

Baptised 1829 - Abergwili
Carmarthenshire
Died 1881
Stockton on Tees
County Durham

=
m. 1860
Escomb
County Durham

Isabella Bird

Born 1840
New Thornley
County Durham
Died 1895 - Middlesbrough
North Yorkshire

Caleb Burgess

Died 1914
Sedgefield
County Durham

m. 1882
Durham
=

Alice Esther Lewis

Born 1876
Middlestone Moor
County Durham
Died 1964 - Guisborough
North Yorkshire

Margaret Lewis

Born 1871
Witton Park
County Durham
Died 1909 - West Hartlepool
County Durham

Mary Valentine Thomas

Primrose Vera
Jennie Lewis

Born 1918

Violet Margaret
Brittannia Lewis

Born 1911

Rachel Lewis

Born 1864
West Hartlepool
County Durham
Died 1939 - Low Fell
County Durham

**William Francis Lewis
(aka Frank)**

Born 1869
Darlington
County Durham
Died 1940
Abergwili
Carmarthenshire

=
m. 1901

Mary Isabel Lewis

Born 1909

Mary (Polly) Lewis

Born 1862
Witton Park
County Durham
Died 1951 - Throckley
Northumberland

Hetty Maud Louise Lewis

Born 1908

Elsie Stonehouse

Born 1904
Hull, East Yorkshire
Died 1955 - Billingham
County Durham

Mabel Inez Hopley

=
m. 1930

**Kenneth Arthur
Leslie Lewis**

Born 1905
Llandebie
Carmarthenshire
Died 1991
Swansea
West Glamorgan

=
m. 1955
Stockton on Tees

Susan Lewis

Wm James Leslie Lewis

Born 1904

Anthony William Lewis

John Francis
Denton Lewis

Born 1903

Further reading

A History of Wales 1815-1906: D Gareth Evans, University of Wales Press Cardiff (1989)

Merthyr Tydfil Iron Metropolis – Life in a Welsh industrial town: Keith Strange, The History Press Ltd (2005)

Reminiscences of a Workhouse Medical Officer: Joseph Rogers MD, T Fisher Unwin (1889)

Welsh cattle drovers: Richard Moore-Colyer, Landmark Collector's Library (2006)

The Local records of Stockton and the Neighbourhood: Thomas Richmond, republished by Patrick & Shotton (1972)

Witton Park – Forever Paradise: compiled by Ken Biggs Keith Belton and Dale Daniel, printed by Lintons Printers, Co. Durham (2002)

Cast in Paradise: Howard Chadwick, Trafford Publishing (2005)

The Boer War: Thomas Pakenham, Random House (1979)

With the flag to Pretoria Volumes I and II, Harmsworth brothers (1900 & 1901)

The Great Boer War: Sir Arthur Conan Doyle, Smith, Elder & Co London (1900)

Social conditions, status and community 1860-c.1920 edited by Keith Laybourn, Sutton Publishing (1997)

The Perfect Summer – dancing into shadow England in 1911: Juliet Nicolson, John Murray (2006)

Remembrance of a riot – the story of the Llanelli Railway Strike Riots of 1911: John Edwards (1988)

Looking around Llanelli with Harry Davies, Llanelli Town Council (1985)

A Llanelli Chronicle, complied by Gareth Hughes (1984)

Life at the ICI: Memories of Working at ICI Billingham: editor Margaret Williamson, Printability Publishing Ltd (2008)

www.workhouses.org.uk